THE SONG
IN THE SILENCE

By
Cheryl Silvera

iUniverse, Inc.
New York   Bloomington

The Song in the Silence

A memoir of beauty from the ashes of sexual abuse and bipolar disorder

iUniverse books may be ordered through booksellers or by contacting:

iUniverse
1663 Liberty Drive
Bloomington, IN 47403
www.iuniverse.com
1-800-Authors (1-800-288-4677)

Because of the dynamic nature of the Internet, any Web addresses or links contained in this book may have changed since publication and may no longer be valid. The views expressed in this work are solely those of the author and do not necessarily reflect the views of the publisher, and the publisher hereby disclaims any responsibility for them.

ISBN: 978-1-4401-3623-8 (sc)
ISBN: 978-1-4401-3624-5 (ebk)

Printed in the United States of America

iUniverse rev. date: 05/29/2009

ACKNOWLEDGEMENTS

The author wishes to thank all those who encouraged me to write this book. I am immensely grateful for my darling sister and friend Grace Silvera who always believed in me and champions everything I do. To Shelley Flannery, my fellow tea lover, who read the first draft and saw promise. To Bevole Mills, my prayer warrior and Linneth Dean, my childhood friend and a rock of encouragement.

DEDICATION TO VALDEZ
My champion 1960-1977

I remember you
The way you held my hand.
I remember you
You were my champion, well-mannered.
I remember you
How with patience you taught me cricket the game.
I remember you
During puberty, you cried with shame,
I remember you
When your chest protruded, the boys called you names.
I remember you
When you reached the height of six feet,
you had only one foot.
I remember you
You had joy and gratitude that your sisters from
Cancer were spared.
I remember you
How in our joys and sorrows you shared.
I remember you
Captain of the cricket team,
I remember you

You were the head-boy at your school.
I remember you
Captain of the soccer and table-tennis teams.
I remember you prankster of fame
I remember you
When your voice broke and squeaked.
I remember you
How everyone listened when you spoke.
I remember you
When you said good-bye,
I remember you
When you said "meet me in the sky".
I remember you
How the green Bible you bought,
told about the God you sought.
I remember you
You are never far from my thoughts.
I remember you my brother.
I remember the promise you asked for, the one I gave
*That on **That Day in the sky,** we'll be together,*
*with **Our Father**, and never die.*
I remember you.

INTRODUCTION

By The Author

This book is written for every 'good-girl' and 'good-boy' that may feel they are alone with the recall of horrible past ordeals. It is a short book to facilitate all those like me who havwe trouble concentrating and getting through a full length book. Its pages are designed to bring you comfort as it underscores you are not alone. I am not particularly fond of telling secrets as some may see it, but in honoring the lives of those who are experiencing trials. Here, I share a blanket of darkness and a bleakness of future that left me without a sense of belonging. While it was robbing me of knowing who I was and what I expected of myself, it was sometimes followed by circuitously reliving of the instant and the surrounding of the perpetration of these ordeals. The recall of unspeakable events caused me to think I was a classic victim. Therefore, for years my life was constructed around the erroneous thought that I was not good enough nor was I of worth to one single soul, hence, I could not justify my existence, I believed I was the invisible person.

I feared that at any time I could and would end my life. This fear was also beckoning me to enter the glorious meadow that was filled with yellow flowers. In my childhood fantasy I would be able to blank my mind and read, lying in the grass looking up into the clear blue skies. Among the yellow flowers and being totally alone the aching need to proclaim my innocence and to ask... why was I the one scorned by society? Because I could not justify my existence so self-offing was a viable solution and a welcome sweetness. I thought it offered me a way out of my misery. But just then, the God who told me that He loved me, so much so that even the very hairs on my head were numbered... and that He knew me before I was formed in the womb... Fear that no one cared and the burden of a hurting victim gradually subsided. Ever so slowly my perception was switched! It changed my life from that of being sucked down by a blob of oozing, sucking nothingness to one of peace and greater strength enough to stand as a fighter and a survivor.

It is with boldness and confidence that I to say to the men and women who are hurting yet who chose to embark on a spiritual journey, those who feel as the apostle Paul, that 'there is a thorn in the flesh.' That thorn may not be removed as Paul found out because you cannot turn back time to erase the reality of past hurts, reality must be faced. I cannot undo my rape and sexual abuse nor can I undo my brain chemicals to drive away the bipolar disorder. I can however manage my symptoms and find help to place each trauma in the light of recovery. Recollections that threatened to kill any future by playing the scenarios over and over in my head, the reliving of those horrible experiences that left me with vivid flashbacks and a debilitating sense of doom. It was through this mélange of confusing emotions that I purposed to find myself again.

For the children of God, we often find no support from spiritual leaders who beat around the bush because of their lack of knowledge of the subject, so they leave us sometimes worse off that when we started sharing with them to obtain guidance. For them to help us leave our condition of hopelessness and perplexity behind, we must ask for them to research the subject so they can help and we must assert that we are people of faith and not "a 'second class' faith believer".

Defying all customary laws of morality and principles of nature, I endured a mind-numbing trauma before I was thirteen years old to triumph in the victory of survival at age thirty-nine; an ordeal that God saw me through. In this book you will experience the indomitable hope and conferences of a new life. Now, He is helping me in cleansing the resulting defiling and unbearably destructive thoughts. The thing for me in writing a memoir of the experiences of triumph over compound suffering is planting the seed of the good work of eradicating stigma by sharing our stories. Wanting others to accept you with your myriad of other behavior is not a selfish thing. When I accept you, and accept you me, then we are less likely to experience stigma towards others unlike ourselves. Bipolar Disorder, the feeling of uselessness and the trauma stemming from childhood sexual abuse will not be the end of me! The reverberation of the memory of healing and the effects of living with the stigma of mental illnesses was my heritage, but through it all I found a magnificent voice.

This composition is entitled "The Song in the Silence," and is synonymous of my perception of God's compassion as he leads me through the valley of the shadow of death. My writing tells of peace and knowledge, the ingredients of reassurance that led me to the portal of self assessment and a design of restructuring.. I speak plainly of the effects of Post Traumatic Stress Disorder mixed with Bipolar Disorder and tumultuous ebbs and flows that begged me to end it all. For so long my life seemed to exist in sound bites, brief moments of clarity and productivity mixed with or followed by chaos and confusion that brings its own dirty blanket that closed out all light and settled heavily on me with sticky sweet depression. A depression that lures me to all things, see all things wrong with me while it beckons to an even deeper darkness of death. The instruments portrayed in this book are dear to me, they represent my openness to learn and appreciation of new knowledge.

When you come right down to it, these instruments clashed, clanged, soothes or excited, they aptly reflect how I see the world around and my life. My life is colorful from years of art study and practice. It is dramatic and weird, peppered by acceptance of living in my present existence through which I must survive with a firm sense of my giftedness and potentials. I feel so confident that the word of God which gave me comfort will also comfort you, so I am sharing some of my favorite promises from the New International Version (NIV) of the Bible. They are interspersed throughout emphasizing God's words of acceptance and coping that reflects each stage of my life as I became acquainted with Him.

This book, a labor of my heart and triumph of the wandering mind, reflects my curiosity and artistic inspiration by emphasizing early mid eastern musical instrument that evokes the emotions that underlie the theme that God is the source of strength and gladly assures me as the song in the silence of the blackness of my life. It is God who is and leads us to the source of all help, starting with our words about ourselves.

This testimonial gives an advocates point of view on the topic of Bipolar Disorder and sexual abuse and how it affects the believer's worship, family life and relationships. The focus of the two topics featured in this work aren't ones we typically discuss in church. While sharing my story in church one man was so moved that he informed me that his wife had suffered from bipolar for thirty years and every time she came out of the hospital the church shunned her. She was a faithful follower and that went on until her death. I am vocal about the subject and keep asking for prayers and visits when in the hospital. Not all others are so lucky; they suffer in silence or are seen as somehow other than blessed. In these last days, we ought to recognize what the Lord means when He commissions us to take care of each other.

Table of Contents

THE SONG
IN THE SILENCE

Chapter 1

The Song in the Silence

AN INTRODUCTION TO GOD AS THE MUSIC IN MY SOUL

Answer me when I call to you, O my righteous God. Give me relief from my distress; be merciful to me and hear my prayers as you promised in Psalms. 4:2 (NIV). It took a kind pastor to send me to another for pastoral counseling before I could say the words

"My name is Cheryl and I am an incest survivor". Those ten words were perhaps the most powerful combination I had uttered in my young life. My perception, as described by those words, was communicating a concept that I had never thought possible before. The concept that I had a hand in shaping a hopeful future for myself was an empowering one.

This for me was the start of an immensely tear jerking journey on the road to healing and recovery. This was a bondage breaking moment that was not lost on me. It's not possible to forget the moment when an albatross is pried from your shoulders. The load shedding came in part because I was one of many who shared that experience. I had held the misconception that I was uniquely alone with this experience. Not so!

At this stage in my life I already a baptized Christian, that is one who is submerged in a public declaration of complete trust and dedication to God. This was important to me because

I had started reading the bible in earnest and enjoyed it for its anthropological context as I completed my studies in graduate school despite the fact that I had not attended church in over twenty years. Before my baptism I had no one to account to for my restless condition, no one to see the the agony in my eyes as painful flashback racked my entire body. I could hide from the world when I wanted to and emerge when I felt safe. All this had changed with joining a church. I had cast my lot and found that the gamble was more than I was prepared for. No one told me I would be lost in church, struggling to hide my condition and desperately to assimilate.

The tension and dichotomy was so powerful I thought I would snap. I did not know what was wrong with me but I knew I was not as the others. I found myself living a complete lie and embroiled in a disappointment in church. I questioned my expectations but not my trust in God. I was living with a shame that was so deeply entrenched that it blocked the flow of blessings I could receive. Despite the fact that we had weekly testimony and prayers at church, mine was not a burden I could share. Or so I thought, until now with the writing of this manuscript.

Outwardly, I was a pleasant, even happy person who was considerate of others. I was active in the church; giving of the talents God had gifted me. I couldn't understand why I was so horrifically ashamed all the time. What was I ashamed of? I was following God's plan for my life and I was engaged in Bible study and prayers. Through clinical counseling and group participation, I learned that anger, despair, grief, rage and hopelessness are all symptoms of this atrocity of sexual abuse, a trauma that must be addressed and surrendered to God to find peace and reclaim self. When I found out from the clinicians that there was a scientific factor that explained this mess of a life it made more sense to me than any local remedy of name calling had ever done. Later I will tell you of a laughably ridiculous diagnosis given to my parents when

I was seventeen. With investigation an following its natural chain of discovery I later found that there are appropriate avenues of expression and healing, like group therapy, counseling and good friends where these matters can be spoken of without feeling self-conscious. I still could not understand why the church did not want to hear. Please don't get me wrong my interest was not that of getting on a soap box and declaring myself the most wronged person in history. No, my desire was one of finally belonging and sharing in tolerance and understanding with my new "friends."

The zooming highs and lows and the racing thoughts of bipolar disorder compounded these symptoms of trauma for me and I am hoping that it may not apply to every reader. Sometimes there were such bursts of energy that made it possible for me to organize my life and attend school, even attending graduate school and to work intermittently. Those days were peppered with weeks when I could not get out of bed.

This was a time when I would sleep around the clock, not able to take care of myself. It wasn't until I was thirty-nine that I was diagnosed with bipolar disorder.

I would like to share with you an entry from my journal dated February 24, 1996. "Today and last night I cried for the child that was abused. I cried for the hurting child that resides inside me. My child-self. I have come to realize that that child was wronged and hurt. I realize that the child struggled and survived. I am learning to admire that child, to attribute all courage and admiration to that child. That it is OK to weep with that child not for the child. It does not need my pity. The child needs my love. I need to respect, admire and love that child. The choices the child made were choices of survival.

I survived because the child survived. The child is the whisper of the strength that is within me. All the setbacks and triumphs of that chills are mine as well. If that child is to be set free, if that child is to be accorded all the pleasures of living, laughter, joy, sorrow, tears and love, I have to help. I have to find a place, a safe place for that child. Not in my heart locked away, but set free on the journey of life and love, in relationships and employment and living at its fullest.

I have also come to realize that the child has grown into a cultured educated woman. Far removed from the limitations set for her. I have come to the conclusion that I will not overwork myself to prove good citizenship at church. Oftentimes we use a super-eager willingness to prove we belong and gain approval, but I will stop all such actions. The child does not crave approval to validate her existence. I will, with God's help, learn to give thanks for my mind and body; a divine gift. I am fearfully and wonderfully made." Created to survive.

As an artist we are familiar with combining pigments to produce hues and tones, this method I desperately applied to color my life just right. When one thing did not work I would re-invent myself to discover clarity and purity. My palette knife was my internal machinations. My canvas would be my acceptance by the world I knew. There are many discarded canvases along the way to self discovery. Some pigment were laid on too thick and ended up with cracks. Some oxidized and turned to mud, losing all clarity to become an unpleasant blob. As a spot on humanity. Still others laid on thin and runny becoming a transparent smear. Through all these processes a master hand is needed. I needed the hand of God. I picked up so many interest and disciplines as I sought a distinction of my breathing being. Jumping from profession to profession was also a part of the unrest and uncertainty of my place in this creation. Each time I tried something else I was hoping for instant attachment and commitment that would indicate my purpose in life. It was a long time in coming. I did not know the master was ordering my steps. Through my detours he called me back to Himself and gently guide me along. Because I did not know His voice and purpose I danced to my own drumming. By now I was the reluctant Jepetto trying to create one whom I could love. Me.

As much as I wanted it to, time did not stand still to let me off. In a journal entry – January 1, 2000. "It's a new year and the world is going nuts about this being a new millennium. There are lots of celebrations all over the place. I cancelled going to the celebration at church, as I did not feel a part of it. The reason for my invitation was to decorate the fellowship hall. That was not good enough in my mind I wanted to feel loved and a part of the group. I did not feel that way.

When I told the organizer that I would not be able to attend she pressed me to come in for a few hours to set-up the hall. It was not me she wanted, just my skills. We agreed on a theme for the evening and went shopping together leaving her with full instructions on rendering the theme. But that was not enough for them, my touch was needed to achieve the effect. I was crazed out of my mind wondering what they wanted from me. I was not part of them! I was not in the mood.

You have read of my struggles with my place within my congregation. For so long I have assumed the role of the one with the problem of not understanding others. My frequent absences were not even noticed. I will need to build on what I have as friends and continue to move forward in faith before I lose it. Maybe it will help if I chant this mantra "I am Cheryl and 'I can do all things through Christ who strengthens me.'"

Journal entry – October 8, 2000. " The day is really beautiful. It is nice and bright, full of promises. How I use those promises are up to me. Feel refreshed and ready for the day, but then again it looms as a day that requires too much effort. I sat in the living room for a few moments, even put the radio on. Then the steam just seems to go out of me. I don't want to do anything, not even wash my hair. I know my sister is off today, but I can't seem to get the energy to want to go visit her. The day is so beautiful. I need to find the energy to do things and have a fuller life. The mood stabilizing medications can't do this for me. Only I can with God's help. My life is still dragging on empty. There are no activities to fill my day. This is a long weekend and I have no plans for it. I am afraid to make plans because I may not keep them. Yet there is so much I could do at home to be busy and fulfilled. I need badly to work on my spiritual life."

Journal entry – November 4, 2000. "Things have gone bad with me. I have ended up alone. I have a job an apartment, but no babies, and no husband. I guess I missed my chances. All my decisions have led up to this. I have few connections with the outside world. My religious connections

are broken. If I try to talk about my pain and experiences my dear friends at church shut me up abruptly. After all it is not polite to air your dirty laundry in public. I feel stripped. Now that I am down at the bottom I wonder where I will settle. I am not proud of locking myself away, but there does not seem to be able to figure out myself. I hope I am not mad."

Recovery is possible even with the strength of paranoia and the doubt of depression. The scriptures you have read, heard and wished it were so for you will come leaping alive with promise and meaning for you. The road to recovery means becoming an advocate for yourself and speaking out. Hiding and thinking that a Christian should not be so afflicted is not in the Lord's plan for you. Like you, I have hidden myself in the back-pew as a silent observer. On the other hand I have also held the position as the head deaconess, communications director, church clerk and served where I have been asked. Presently I am the founder of a ministry to encourage "Keeping the faith when Mental Illness Strikes". Being actively involved in church or not, I am not ashamed. Well that is the boldness speaking. I have found that I am not always so assured, but by looking back at all the Lord has done for me and where He has led me, reassures me that inner strength is once again possible because it is born in confidence of who He is. This is a continuous journey of handing over my distress and gaining peace. In this place my 'threshing-floor', here, I am reminded that recovery requires hard work and self-involvement. It is here that I understand that to get rid of the dross I must have a knowledge of all that aches and all that is precious. This is not something easy to do because I did not always know what I was looking for. I did not know myself and did not have a blueprint to tell me my true self as set free by God. That came with searching the scriptures and proving Him.

When my Lord told me that I am wonderfully and fearfully made, in no way did he mean for me to carry the baggage of pervert whose motto was pleasure at all cost. Understanding that led me to an understanding that he will give me 'beauty for ashes' of my life. Wishing it so instantly unfortunately did not happen for me. Recovery is possible, but it takes hard work. To know that I am held tenderly in God's arms is a comfort for me. There are moments when I can't do the work required and in those moments I am sent angels to help lift me up. Had I seen winged creatures I would probably have to add another trauma, no these angels are sometimes my family, a kind doctor, a grocery clerk or simply someone on the street. I know a gift of kindness when I see it.

I am constantly reassuring (reaffirming to some) that I am a worthy person. I have difficulty getting out of bed bogged down by a heavy sleep. It's not possible for me to say my life has suddenly turned into a peach. It's more like a peach with fragments of tooth cracking pits in it. The challenge for me is not to dwell on the fact that I am still affected by my early childhood trauma and the symptoms of Bipolar Disorder. The beauty is that 'the beauty' promised from 'the ashes' is blooming. I suppose there will not be a sense of arriving at perfection, at least not just yet.

Chapter 2

The Song in the Silence

THE SONG, THE BEAT
IS THE ESSENCE
OF MY LIFE

---

*L*et them praise his name with dancing And make music to him with tambourine and harp. Ps. 149:3 (NIV). I sat surrounded by a silence that was punctuated by the sounds of life all around me. Sometimes I thought life was around me but not with me.

I sat, that was then. Now I stand, and move and dance. Now I hear the rhythm, the beat resonating deep from someplace deep within and it is the essence of life Himself within me. The beat surrounds me; it's in tandem with my life. My steps are ordered. My dance is with grace. My body, my heart is moved, led by the beat. The beat is life Himself. The beat is silence; it's a whisper so loud I wonder why others can't hear it.

This beautiful silence and natural beat has replaced a cacophonous noise that lived in me for so long. The noise was created by incest at a tender age and a life long battle with undiagnosed bipolar disorder. Along with other atrocities heaped upon my young head these two almost did me in. They clung tenaciously to me, refusing to let go or allow me a semblance of 'normal' life. They invaded my professional life, my development, my friendships, and offered their ribald commentary on my life. They drove me to the brink of madness.

I often wondered if mad people knew they were mad, because surely they must feel the way I do. Connected to reality but somehow not a part of it. You are on the fringes as an occupant but not a participant of the reality that is observed. Like an extra in a movie, you form a part of the mob scene, disconnected from the main plot but an integral part wandering along, seemingly with a purpose but none existed.

That was my life. I am still not sure where the toll of one ended and the grind of the other began, regardless, both made for a rather tempestuous existence. During recovery the demarcation lines were drawn with the help of my church family, good friends, family and various doctors and therapists. The part that God played in my recovery cannot be minimized. When I first came to Him in the summer of '91, he told me *"For I know the plans I have for you...not to harm you...to give you (shalom)a hope and a future..." Jer. 29:11.* This promise I struggled with for many years while believing it and awaiting its' fulfillment. I will speak of it often in this work. The fact that God is concerned with my well being, to prosper me, an assurance that He will not harm me and that I will have hope and a future. When the sheer magnitude of that promise hit me with full force, I was astounded at the offer and then I issued a challenge for Him to prove it. Through the unstable noise of my pained mind and heart the promise was gifted, I found peace in the form of a sweet silent song in my heart.

I then wondered how I could share this the beat, how to let others know that the beat, the dance was at one with the silence. Then it, the beat, whispered in my heart, *"Take courage! As you have testified about me in Jerusalem, so you must also testify in Rome."* Acts. 23:11. My beat is God. In the noise of my aloneness and tragic condition, He came to me and offered His music.

At first I didn't recognize or accept the song, but he accompanied me with its haunting strains. When I was in shutdown mode, to preserve my sole and sanity, He gave a melody so sweet. When I cried so that the only sound in my head was that of a child that was violated and ripped apart as her body and mind were plundered, He gave his soothing music. Now I know that it was an attempt to separate me from the source of the divine melody. But God made us more than conquerors. Paul said, *"...If God is for us, who can be against?"* *Rom. 8:3.(NIV)*

The music led me and gave me an appearance of gracefulness. It fathered me with its deep resounding Shofar and settled me with its melody. When I was a child it was the melodious harp-like sound of the sackbut. In my early teen years it was it was the jangling sound of the Timbrel. In my late teens it was the clashing of the cymbals. Then it became the organ in my early adulthood. The bells of the high priest interceded for me. He did not quit as I called upon Him. The drummer was in control.

The drummer dwells within me, but is not me. The drummer could have passed from me but he stayed. He stayed and strummed me back to silence from the noise of rage, shame, grief, confusion and flashbacks in which I had no identity. Now I know who I am. I am a child of the King, with a hope and a future. Now I can hear the silence. I can hear the beat.

With the beautiful music in my heart I was able to study at home for my British exams while I waited to become of age to enter college. I was successful at both and earned my degree with second-class honors. I landed a choice job even before I graduated. Both school and work were a tremendous challenge for me. I kept having elating highs and debilitating lows.

During my first year in college I was hospitalized for two weeks in a private hospital. Of this experience I have no memory. All I remember of this was my sister screaming at the sight of me when I asked her to pick up my artwork and drop it off at school for the weekly critique. I do remember that I had been up for a couple nights painting tiny squares to create a sunset. I returned to school with a professor asking me why I was so pale and wanting to know what was the name of my particular complexion, a shade of yellow. Other than that, no one was aware that I was in a psychiatric hospital for two weeks.

There were no further hospitalizations during the four years of school. That would come later. In retrospect I realized that my steps must have been ordered from the beginning. He said, *"Before I formed you in the womb I knew you, before you were born I set you apart..."* Jer. 1:5 (NIV). Before I recognized or accepted the promise in these words I thought the promise would be silenced by the misdeeds directed towards me an attempt to silence the song.

THE SACKBUT OF CHILDHOOD
Know yourself

"For we are God's workmanship, created in Christ Jesus to do good works, which God prepared in advance for us to do." Rom. 2:10 (NIV). I grew upJ on a small island in the middle of the Caribbean Sea that had an emblem of Arawak Indians, the original inhabitants, and a reference to the wildlife, flora and fauna of the land. Those folks were wiped out by Columbus and his crew. A few Negro Slaves and some Indian Peons were introduced. It wasn't until the English in the form of General Venables and Admiral Penn trounced the Spanish ending their one hundred and forty-five years rule that we were gradually set on the road to stability.

As the busiest and main seaport between the new world and the old, Jamaica was ideally situated. Even though it was not the largest island, two other took that top honor, Cuba and Hispaniola. This is where our best friend entered, the swash buckling Henry Morgan was an unlikely hero. He and his pirates defended the island fiercely. Not so long ago, in the eighteenth century, West African slaves were imported to work the sugar-cane fields. After that people kept pouring in. People who came from varying lands for various reasons They came from Asia, Africa and Europe to call that tiny island home. It has been a very painful process that we became citizens as one in this land and are still learning to live as one. Worldwide.

This knowledge of ourselves as a people with our rich heritage as hunters and gathers and later as slaves to free people tells of the strength of a people who may look different from each other but who claimed unity with each other have helped us to survive and thrive . That was the Jamaica I grew up in. A country that gained independence and lowered the Union Jack to raise the flag of black, green and gold one year after my birth. Black for strength, sreen for the fertile land and yellow for sunshine, it was the land of wood, water and sunshine.

As a people to that land, its motto "Out of many, one people" caused all who lived there to feel a sense of belonging. The reasons for our arrival was superseded by the encouragement to be with each other as one people. The Jews, like many immigrants who sought a new life there, started settling in Jamaica in 1663. The name *Silvera* is Portuguese. The family is related to the first Portuguese conquerors of the Iberian Peninsula in the 11th century. All the Jewish families in Portugal adopted names of trees because of the Inquisition. The name Silvera means Blackberry thicket. Sephardic comes from the Hebrew word for Spain. Jews from the region of Spain and Portugal are reffered to as Sephardic Jews. According to Paul in Rev. 21: 9-12 "Anyone who would come into the Bride of the Messiah must necessarily enter through Israel" (Jew or Gentile). "Gentile followers of Yeshua are grafted into the olive tree of remnant Israel". Rom.

11:16-24 I included that bit so there will be no misunderstanding against my claim of my father and his people.

~

Those Portuguese Jews chose the parish of St. Mary (similar to a state in the USA) to settle. That's where I spent my entire developing years. My father was a mixture of these Portuguese Jews and Maroons (African slaves from the hills, including St. Mary). From very early on my father wanted us to be aware of our heritage, but we had no idea what he was talking about. The lack of Synagogues and the fact that he was not a practicing Jew did not help. They were Jews in name only. But somehow it seemed important that we maintained that tradition by remembering who we were. My mother further complicated the matter by introducing her own mixed heritage of Scottish ancestry.

The Jamaican people came from many backgrounds but were one people. That seemed important to our father, that we have a knowledge of our mixed heritage. My father was a tall, statuesque man with a big voice and big ears. He was a gentle man capable of yelling at flag men who let trucks through on fresh macadam when he was in the process of making a road. The macadam was the final step in the process to be spread cooled and tramped down. To walk on this fresh layer was to incur serious burns. This hot macadam had to be cooled and left to set for several hours before being ready for vehicles much less truck. He bellowed at the unfortunate youth, fired him and rehired him the next day with a new task, no flags.

In this world of I-pods and Blackberry's, it's easy to lose track of the fact that most of our original roads were constructed from cow-tracks under the supervision of a brilliant mathematician with minimal formal training. In an age before Computer Assisted Drawing, CAD, V. G

Silvera could calculate as well as any surveyor's instrument. Slopes, angles, vectors and volume had to be calculated by a trusted tape measure, drainage or run-off, shoulder and choice of material to be used were all calculated by one man. He worked for the then Public Works Department, now the National Works Agency. He made roads from St. Andrew to St. Mary, Trovy Hill, Clonmell and Georgia. My father.

～

After a heavy rain, fallen boulders and trees were removed from the tracks of Junction by mules and wagons in time for the rush hour traffic. According to a former Member of Parliament, V. G. Silvera, one of the few Sephardic Jews of Jamaica, was the first Supervisor to be given heavy-duty motorized equipment to complete the job. During his retirement he was called upon to fix the troublesome Hagley Park Road.

～

Mr. Silvera, or Champi (short for champion) as he was called, gladly gave of his life to serve his country wherever he was sent. As long as there were roads to be made or re-engineered he stepped up to his duty. We lived in government houses in various locations for most of our lives. You've heard of the term army-brats; well the phrase road-brats could be coined for his children. The family had to be prepared to move at the urgency of the next job. Next to his family, making roads was his passion.

～

He was well respected in the community and was seen as the harbinger of jobs, tankers of fresh water for the community when there was a drought. Our family and the community could not have survived without him. The respect that the community had for my father would be conferred on us as well. Old men would doff their dusty field hats wringing them as they bid us a good-day. As children we were uncomfortable with this practice and would try to avoid the seniors, but not wanting to hurt their feelings we would try to greet them first and run as fast as we could.

Our country was a Christian community emphasizing that our belief played into our development as individuals and as a country. The only ramification of that fact was the evidence that we were not attached to any religious congregation. When we were very young my mom sent us to keep the pastors company in the local church. The church was across the street and doubled as the library. No adults attended Wednesday prayer meeting so we were sent to give the pastor an audience. Neither my mother nor father attended these services.

My mother was a housewife and skilled in the art of many things. She is very creative and a brilliant cook. The people of the village often called on her when they were sick. She was an excellent seamstress and at one point had her own fabric shop. She made most of our clothes while we were growing up. My mother was determined that we would not be spoiled so she would take us frequently to the ancestral farms in Crescent to camp out for two weeks each summer. She is of short stature, one would say petite, very pretty with a knack of making friends easily. She maintained the stability of our home.

This wasn't easy because my father's job took us from town to town making roads and we had to go with him until the project was finished. Sometimes we would move two or three times in the school year. The sackbut with its soothing harp-like sound kept me through the early years. It kept me when I lived in the beautiful floral fantasy that was the pride of the island, Castleton Gardens. The garden was everything paradise could be, huge palm trees lining the road and a river running through it. Smaller English style gardens with walking paths and large wooded areas with rare trees and shrubs. All guarded over by the high blue-green mountains on either side. Castleton was a true tropical paradise. We lived in a little government house behind the post office, smack in the middle of the garden while my dad built roads.

During those years my song was in my heart, it was always with me, making me happy. This was especially so as I rode pillion to my brother on his red tricycle. Valdez was a year older and was my protector. It was just the two of us for a while before the others came of age to play. We would ride up and down the numerous paths of the garden, his little legs frantically pumping to propel us from adventure to adventure.

We would investigate the huge gum tree and various flora and fauna. All around us were giant trees and perfumed blossoms. Our favorite spot was the frog pond, when we were missing they knew where to find us. We had our own hill; we named it Bunker Hill because we would use the fallen bunker a cusp from the palm tree to glide down the hill. We would do this over and over until we had had enough. Our laughter and squeals would often bring tourists to investigate the sound of such glee. Maybe this bout with nature is what led my brother to buy a bible and without prompting from any human, walked into church and gave his life to God at age fifteen. Preparing the way for others to follow.

The beautiful sackbut was still with me when we left our paradise behind and started over in a new town. Because of our nomadic lifestyle we lived in everything from orange groves to small towns. At one time we had a mule and buggy.

One of our stops was a fair sized town with its pathways shooting off the main road. It was here that I had the nest attack on my song, but it was still there when my brother and I were tossed out of the family home. We sat outside on our suitcases for the better part of the day. I was probably six years old and he was seven and we could not understand why it was happening. Now I know, my mom was battling her own tiger. My song was there when my dad came to get us in his government supplied Land Rover.

Papa came like a knight in shining government supplied armour to protect us, and swooped us away to his office with the cot to sleep the night away until the crisis had passed.

It would be years later before I learned the story of their courtship. She was the pretty new girl staying with relatives in town and he was the local jock. He was on the National circuit playing cricket and was good at it earning him the nick name Champion. He had won his fair lady with a fake faint below her window after she refused to go out with him. She was impressed with his ingenuity in courting her and so she relented.

I arrived on the scene about two years later as the second child of that marriage. A boy had preceded me. They made a handsome couple. My dad was six feet four inches tall and very good-looking. He attributed his good looks to his Maroon ancestry mixed with his Jewish heritage. The Maroons were the hill dwelling dark skinned descendants of the African slaves brought to the island, and the Jews in my father's case were the descendants of the Sephardic Jews that had fled Portugal during the inquision. My family isn't the only Jews on the island as Jamaica was a popular portal when fleeing Europe on their way to the land of the Dutch. My mom's family has tales of Jewish ancestry through her grandmother of the Levy Clan.

My mom is petite with river clear brown eyes and a silky complexion. She is quite handy with a needle and thread and is a good cook. She was the planner of the two. She provided stability during the incessant moving. She quickly made friends and established routines. Where ever we went she was often she was often seen as the go to person.

By the time we were left on our suitcases to await our father, my mom had reached the end of her rope. All that moving had taken its toll. The night we were taken to my dad's quarters was the second attack on my song. This time in the form of foisting on us the role of pawns. I am sure my dad did the best he could, with my brother in the crook of his arm and me cushioned on the fat of his stomach. He was clearly uncomfortable to have us so physically close in an embarrassing intimacy. His stomach should have been a safe and comfortable place for me, but with each breath he took to expel a sonorous snore, I was in danger of being tossed. Sleep was fitful that night.

From that day on, the thought that it is only a matter of time before I am kicked aside fear rode side by side with my song. During those years of the Sackbut I had no idea that my song was singing *"...God has said, Never I will leave you; never will I forsake you." Heb 13:5.* Soon we moved again. My image of my brother Valdez as my hero was emblazoned on my heart with his kindly protection towards his sisters.

We were sent to live with a distant relative, so my mom could make her sojourn to America. We were sorry to leave our familial unit behind but excited at the prospect of living on a working farm. Most animals on the farm we had only seen in books or from afar. There were huge skirted sows, ducks, goats, cows, bulls and chickens.

As the miles closed and we approached the tip of the map, the landscape changed. The hills flattened and the grass grew taller, so tall it was called savannah land. Everything was reddish brown with very little shelter from the sun. The day we arrived there was a storm with gale like winds that blew down the fully-grown plum tree in the back yard and pelted the tall grass in a fury of nature. We watched from the windows in a heightened state of excitement, with our mother assuring us that everything was going to be all right. No sooner had our mother left than we were trained to take care of the animals and the peanut crop. My job along with my brother was to take the herd of cows, before daybreak, to fetch them water from the wells. I had never seen a well before except in books and they always had a stone surround with a rope dangling from a wooden coiling system. Imagine my shock to find a hole in the ground as little else than an obscene disruption of grass to announce its presence. One was expected to fling a bucket in the opening and haul up water. I remember crying and lying on my belly to keep from falling in. My brother took pity on me and hauled the water after that first attempt. I am sure he must have been as scared as I was after all he was only a year older.

He also took over the herding of the goats when I proved inept at that as well. One was supposed to drive the goats along a chosen path from a safe distance behind them; somehow I always end up being chased by them.

After our morning exertions would come breakfast of peg-bread and a cup of dandelion tea, eaten in the buttery. The buttery was a building of three rooms in a row. The first room was an enclosure that housed the kitchen with its alter of waist high rocks to form an open stove. The middle room housed feed and grain; it was here that tobacco leaves and herbs were dried hanging from the rafters with a small smoking fire to keep out the moisture. The third was open on three sides and was a sort of gazebo. We ate here rain or shine.

A few yards from the gazebo was a standpipe with a pool of water where the ducks would gather. Those ducks were nasty and fierce. They would fight you for your food. The domestic pigs would also water at the standpipe. We soon found out that pigs liked to eat bars of soap. All our allowance was used to buy toiletries despite the fact that our parents sent those items in abundance. When we left our soap in the outdoor bathroom and the pigs got to it, my brother would replenish our supplies without a lecture. Candies and toys were unheard of when you had to be sensible.

It was my big brother who came to the rescue again when he wrote to our mother to come and get us because half our hair was gone from ringworm and we were dining on Purina pig chow to stay alive. She heeded the call and speedily plucked us from the mercilessly harsh winds at nights where one wall was taken out of our bedroom to make way for further expansion to the house. He stood up for something he believed and he was my hero. That was my image of what a big brother should be a hero. He always will be my hero.

Chapter 3

The Song in the Silence

THE TIMBREL YEARS

Clarity and peace

" *T*he mind controlled by the Spirit is life and peace...Rom. 8:6 (NIV). Just as the tremolos jangling sound of the timbrel jars you with its emotions, so too were my early teenage years. That was the worst time of my life. I had survived my preteen years of being excavated over and over again. I already told you that my folks were pillars of our close knit community. My father's job took him away from us frequently.

∿

My folks were very busy doing what parents worldwide do to provide for their young ones. My mother was off to America seeking a better life for us. She came home every six months. My dad was busy building his roads and he no longer took us with him. To solve their problem they hired a guardian/housekeeper.

∿

Those degenerates who trawled for me did not seem to know that I was not theirs to excavate to plunder and condemn. I didn't hear my song when He whispered, *"Jesus wept."*

∿

At some point my song must have been in full swing because we moved again, but not before the first brilliant manifestations of my illness appeared. Whatever my mind conceived I was able to bring to fruition, the first blush of my creativity and imagination as a means of coping emerged. I had a tiny dolls-wear shop that the boys of the neighborhood constructed for me as a platform made of bramble and thatched with coconut fronds. I would use bits of found material; everything from old socks to sleeves of old garments, to fashion exotic garments for the dolls of the girls in my neighborhood. They would bring their dolls to be measured and fitted and I would charge them for my services. Someone had shared with my mom that they thought I was creative and that she should nurture it. That she did by giving me tiny battery operated sewing machines, embroidery starter kits, knitting needles with instruction and my beloved paint and paper. The products for my tiny shop was the cumulative knowledge of these skills my mama taught me. The proceeds of this venture were used to shop for more materials to create better outfits. When I wasn't in school I could be found in my shop outside our home plying my needle. I must have lost interest when the mania wore off because I have no idea what became of this lucrative venture.

～

It was also here, where the ancestral farm was within short walking distance, that my body began its alarming development. It was torture being a little girl in a body that looked like a woman's: every lusty unscrupulous male thought their eyes should be focused ten inches below my chin. I was so mortified that I took to ripping up old sheets and binding them so tightly that there was hardly anything to see. The white cotton cone shaped bras of the day did not exactly help in concealing. I had more than most women I knew and I kept looking to see if I was normal. My mom was forced to buy me a full sized bra and to seek expert advice on this alarming growth. The doctor by the sea ten miles away prescribed a stop growth of nightly salve of a fowl smelling stuff that evoked the farm smell of hot chicken dung. The salve didn't work because my breast continued their rapid growth. It wasn't long before I took to binding them even more tightly, but they refused to be contained.

Not long after this we moved to a little property all our own that my mom purchased with her American money. This, our own land had a small house that my mom expanded to accommodate us all in comfort and style modeled after the American ranch style house. It was a thing of beauty in the hills of St. Mary with a view of the Port Maria beach twenty-odd miles away and was prone to the dangers of thrashing hurricane winds blowing in from the sea. It was perfect for us to be on the "old road" with the swishing of vehicles occurring on the "new road" my father helped to build. We were home at last and no longer at the bidding of the government to move here or there. We were a family at peace and ready to make new friends in this most rural hill dwelling in a genteel manner. I met my best friends Angella and Linneth there.

We had left my guardian's brothers behind but my half-brother arrived. He arrived with his battered suitcase and wild, angry eyes. He was tall, skinny, twenty-four and wore a beard. He looked like a duplicate of J.J. from Good Times. He was so light skinned that he was most like our mother in complexion. He had a big afro with a cap slanted to the side and clothes we were not familiar with. We lived humbly and he came on the scene with all flash and anger and an attitude that the world owed him a favor, called a chip on the shoulder. Looking at him the four of us children did not know that my parents had rescued him by night from sure imprisonment. Where he came from he was the resident bully. There was talk that he was rescued from a sure arrest for the abuse he had heaped on his grandmother and atrocities to others. The police had visited him quite a few times and it was decided that that his latest breach of the law was the last straw, whatever it was. My mother's son and apt pupil of my father he came to live with us to be genteel and to experience a home with his parent, my mom.

My dad welcomed him and took him under his wings. He sat up nights teaching him math then accounting. The glow of the kerosene lamp with its neatly trimmed wick spreading its message of "home sweet home" would soon become a misnomer, but how were we to know that. When my dad thought this evil seed was ready, he got him a job at his place of business then forgot about him. My dad's duty was done. Actually, looking back at it I realize my dad was quite magnanimous to have taken on another man's grown child as he did, but that was the kind of man he was.

The tough years, surviving incest

I cried out to God for help; I cried out to God to hear me...You kept my eyes from closing; I was too troubled to speak Ps.77: 1,4 (NIV).

It should have been a joyous experience with an older half-brother close at hand, even older than my beloved big brother, but it was not. From the moment he arrived he was sullen, mean and demanding. He treated us younger ones like his slaves, ordering us about. We kept hearing the phrase "give him time to adjust." There were constant fights of us against him, when he wasn't beating us up he was inciting a riot. My mom and dad were again at their business of providing for us. There was no one to rescue us from the wild one. Then began his nocturnal visits to my bedroom.

~

My half brother was the miner that would tear down the beams and dry up the vein of my well-being and, still, he excavated for the song in my soul. He couldn't touch my soul, which was off limits to him. He touched everything else. He contaminated me with an incurable shame by planting his replica within me. To that my song said, *"No army shall stand against you, I will vanquish your foes, and pluck your shame from among you."*

The timbrel rose in crescendo as I too swelled and grew with my half-brother's unholy seed. I kept on growing as the circuit court judge made his decision. I grew even bigger as the government dragged their feet. At the final hearing I arrived at the courthouse there was a huge crowd gathered, among them were reporters for various newspapers. I felt my thirteen-year-old knees buckle as I walked up the seeming endless outside steps to the courtroom on the second floor, trying to pretend that I was not there. With a glance I looked down at veritable mob scene. I didn't know there were that many people in town. The case was brought before the magistrate behind closed door, where she decided to terminate the pregnancy. I grew until it was almost time for the replica's natural entrance to this world. Then the court decreed that it should be expelled from my body.

Again I was chauffeured around in a government vehicle, this time it was a police jeep. They took me to the University Hospital where a police stood guard while the thing was induced to arrive early with foot long needles in my distended belly. After hours, or was it days later, the still, lifeless replica appeared. It was whisked away, but not before I saw that it was a boy. Not one family member was allowed to be with me during this ordeal. Recently my mother told me that administrators asked her to leave so she would not hear my screams.

After a short stay in the hospital I was returned to my home. This time my mother and I traveled by taxi because the government's job was over and we were now left to fend for ourselves. We were no longer their concern. Upon alighting from the taxi a well-intentioned neighbor greeted me with a copy of the national newspaper I had missed during my enforced absence. The news had made the front page. Not by name, but who needed a name in a village and town of that size.

I awoke from my faint in the gutter, a fitting place I thought at the time, to the curious crowd and the compassionate eyes of my long time friend, my own full brother. That was the first time I saw love, pure and clean, but I did not recognize it. I was thirteen. Three years later my brother died of cancer. I never saw that look again. I never looked; a veil was over my eyes. It was a veil that was woven from shame and mistrust. I couldn't trust to look.

I know I will see it again. He asked me, on his deathbed, to meet him in Heaven. He had heard my song.

'I will set my angels to camp around you," the Lord said. He must have. I gave up my bed and moved away with my pregnant friend to a hastily constructed hut by a small stream in the woods. She needed someplace to stay and we lived too close to her family. My house was not a good idea because everyone knew I was a bad influence. My friend and I built the hut from coconut fronds on the sides and top. We made two beds from the large dried leaves of the banana tree. We cooked smoky food by day and read Mills & Boon romance by campfire at night. We washed our clothes in the little stream, which was no more than tickle. We would dry the clothes on the roof of our misshapen hut.

We read through the night because we were scared of the night sounds and it gave us a good reason to have the fire going, it kept the shadows at bay. We spent most of our waking time gathering twigs for a pile that was higher than our beds. We also spent a great part coaxing the banana trees to let us have their dried leaves for our beds. Each day we would pile on more leaves and still it was uncomfortable at night.

I was insensitive to the fact that my siblings were going nuts wondering where I was. They had no idea if this was another of my attempts to run away. Oh, I had packed brown shopping bags many times. I just had nowhere to go so I stayed. We lived in our hut for about a week until my sisters found us by following the smoke from our campfire. The little darlings were so proud of themselves; they had found us when no one else could. Living and playing in the bush create good scouts. They were proud of themselves for excellent tracking skills and we were proud that we had erected a hut on the bank of a little stream and that we furnished it from the woods where we were self sufficient.

~

We fed them and sent them away with the promise not to tell the people of the district where we were. They did not squeal just yet, the smoky undercooked food was bribe enough. They complained with each bite they took, berating our lack of culinary skills with the open flame. They broke their promise and told my brother and his friends where we were before we could move camp. They descended on our hut with machetes in hand and demolished in minutes what had taken us days and hours to build. We had no choice but to return home with my brother and his friends calling us all kinds of fool and telling us how lucky we were that some stranger had not harm us.

How long I would have stayed there had we not been found is a thought I will never have to contemplate. Again, potential catastrophe was averted because He had kept His promise. A promise I never knew He had made. My friend was rescued by the father of her unborn child and taken away in marriage. They must have heard the music. Today they are a family of five worshipping the maker of the music together. They worship with the same fervor and in the same church and on the same day as my brother had done.

We learned our lessons from our camping experience. The first one was to never make your bed from banana leaves without first removing the center stalks if you want a restful sleep. Secondly, never make your cook-fire with green twigs, because it smokes too much and not enough flame to actually cook by. And finally, have the good sense to move deep into the woods by swallowing your fears.

The timbrel years were also a time of giving and sharing. It's jangle and bang was the awakenings of greater curiosity and compassion. The sea also reminds me of the timbrel when it rolls to a soft gentle sigh. The Caribbean Sea with its blue-green depths and tiny white caps as it glitters in the noon day sun is marvelous to behold, and was a lure for me. I would ride the bus for twenty-odd miles to go sit in solitude on the beach. I had learned that after the fishermen had left you could have the beach all to yourself. The entrance from the sea was partially block by a tiny reef island that provided visual relief from the water with its trees and shrubs. My beach stretched for almost a mile in that particular cove and was the perfect vantage point for me to watch the gentle waves as they brushed up on the glistening pebbles. Their slate-gray color would shine brilliantly in the glaring sunlight.

From my vantage point under the almond trees and grape trees along the water's edge, I too was caressed by the gentle lapping sound and shimmering jewel-like sparkles that capped the waves. The best time was around noon when the sun was high and all the colors were in full glory. Before then I hadn't realized that there were so many shades of green. I was inspired to paint. I acquired a watercolor set and muddied many a seascape. None of my paintings were ever to my satisfaction.

"I will keep your foot from kicking against the prick," He said. He must have. I guess I was bait for any vagabond that chanced upon my solitude on the beach. I never saw a soul. Except for my mother. Once she took the bus twenty miles and followed me there. I heard the crunch of footsteps and was jarred out of my reverie. I saw with relief that it was my mom. She sat and talked with me for a long time then took me to dinner at a restaurant. For the first time she asked me to share why I was so unhappy. She should have known, so I didn't tell her. We wept there on the beach, she because she could never again reach me, and me because I had lost a little girl when I was thirteen. Myself. She made me promise never to return alone again. I never did.

~

I am glad I had sampled the smooth water on my bare skin before she found my hideout on the beach. That's another of my treasure memories. My family and I returned many times to that beach. I would always sit under the almond trees, avoiding the sun. It was never the same as my solitude, and that phase soon passed.

Chapter 4

The Song in the Silence

THE CYMBAL YEARS

Recognize your achievements

"Y ou let men ride over our heads; we went through the fire and water, but you brought us to a place of abundance. Ps. 66:12 (NIV)

The timbrel years continued with its ebb and flow and gut wrenching wails only to be replaced by the jarring clashing cymbal. They clashed and they reverberated, only to clash again. So I wailed, so I wept. I did not hear my song, but He must have said, "My peace I leave with you."

"Bald head, stocking head," followed the laughing jeers or little children barely younger than me. Their voices came to me through the fog on a clear sun shiny day. It was ninety degreed in the shade and I was walking down the main road on my way to town a couple miles away. What was my mission , I can't remember. It was one of the few times I ventured from my self-imposed isolation with my pale pasty skin and head shave down to the scalp. I was thin as a reed and I looked neither right nor left. My entire focus was keeping upright and not fainting because of the eyes on me.

I had cropped my hair to its very kinky roots trying to sheer off my shame. It only brought me more attention, the very thing I was trying to escape. The children's mocking taunts and the platter of their bare feet slapping the hot asphalt followed me for awhile until they gave up. I never looked back. I never looked back or sideways in those days, just straight ahead. I knew that I could only go forward if I wanted to keep my sanity. I did not speak much those days either. What was there to say. I was now, simply, dead man walking. On to my execution by society and the scornful sneers of those around me. Nothing to talk about, nothing to live for.

Forward to what I didn't know. How could I have known I was moving through the cymbal years to the Shofar years? "When you are weak I will be your strength," He said. He was my strength and I didn't even know it, then.

The mighty reverberation that follows the sharp collision of cymbals was what awoke me each time I would pass out in a dead faint. My swooning would occur at the most inopportune moments. I would faint on the steps of the library. I would faint in the middle of the street. I would faint on the sidewalk, anywhere. I didn't know they were anxiety attacks. The doctors didn't know that either.

To get to the bottom of the swooning our family doctor recommended that I be tested at government psychiatric hospital in the big city. Bellevue was the most ugly, most rundown edifice my eyes had ever beheld. The grouping of dilapidated buildings with their guarded gates and meandering patients were a scary encounter. The guards and a gate were quite unnecessary because there were large gaps where the residents had cut holes in the fence to escape. I was glad to be walking between my mom and dad because I was very afraid to seeking treatment in such a place. Somehow having my shoulder brush against my parents bodies was comforting. It was long established that I was a magnet for the insane. They would seek to get real close to me or to touch me. I was told by my friends not to be afraid of them because they could smell my fear. It didn't work for us this day as one of the mentally ill jumped before us , grabbed my right breast and was chased off by my dad. I was now more convinced than ever that I was meant to be chattel of some unseen foe. No one could possibly have such bad luck

We were asked to return with my hair washed but not dressed. Again we walked pass sightless eyes in various states of dementia to arrive at a tiny office, bare except for a beeping blinking machine with wires hanging. We were interviewed and then I was fitted with the wires with little red disks attached at the ends. I started giggling thinking I must look a fright.

The machines were turned on and a little black pen started across the graph paper, the machine was spitting out what it thought was in my head. But still they didn't find my song. Back to the little office we went for another interview. A Cat scan was needed, they said, we don't have the equipment on the island, get her help where you can. The doctor took one more look at my pale, pasty skin and pronounced that during my frequent fainting spells I could have been suffering from overexposure to ultra violet rays that were not filtered by my skin.

The incredulous diagnosis was that my blood was overheated which caused a rush of blood to my head and caused me to swoon. Remedy? Wear long sleeved shirts, hats, carry an umbrella and stay out of the sun. That was just fine with me since it gave me even more reason to remain indoors.

I stayed indoors, inactive for so long that my muscled near atrophied. I would walk to the clothesline to hang the wet laundry and fall over. I would stub my toe on a loose pebble and fall over. I wasn't swooning as much anymore but I sure was hitting the deck pretty often, we all agreed that I was colossally uncoordinated. That was just fine with me; I would just stay indoors where I couldn't embarrass myself or my family.

"I know the plans I have for you," He said. So the cymbals clashed and pulled me with its sound. I did my duty and it was my pleasure to venture to parents conference to see how my siblings were faring in school. I signed their sick notes, gave permission for parties and trips and watched over them. I watched them like a hawk. No one was going to mess with these chicks under my care. They would not endure what I did. I would stay on watch; I wouldn't let my guard down. I had to know where they were at all times.

It was a source of joy. It never was a burden. I was fourteen years old. I started caring for them before I graduated High school. I was taken out of private school and placed in a government school to spare me the shame. Yet we went to the same town. I got off the bus before they did. They would wait for me at an agreed spot and we would all travel home again. We did this over and over; they were my buffer, my joy. They indulged me when I wanted to walk part of the twenty miles home. They indulged me when bus after bus passed by and still I wasn't ready to board one. We walked for miles and then the last bus left us still walking along the sugarcane fields. They couldn't indulge me any more when an ambulance stopped at dusk and offered us a ride home. We took it. They didn't tell that it was my fault that the entire village was waiting at the town clock with torches made from kerosene in an old rum bottle.

The sea of torches, made from bottles holing kerosene with rags tucked in tightly, greeted us as the ambulance let us out. There was yelling and screaming and hugs and tears for our safe return. Our closet neighbors had supported my mother by walking miles to the clocktower in the town. Still my siblins didn't tell, but my mother guessed. I was a bad influence, I put nature and escape above safety. They were instructed not to wait for me again. Soon my mom left again for America and it was my turn to get up early and fix us all lunches for school. It was my turn to come home early and make the dinner and wash the clothes.

The ironing and cleaning I left for the weekend. The ironing was a big job. You had to starch the blue cotton uniforms and fold the pleats just so as you press them with an iron filled with glowing charcoal. My brother's white shirt and daddy's clothes needed special attention. The cleaning was done by smearing red Rexo floor polish on the wooden planking and buffing it with half of a coconut husk. The buffing would release the fresh cedar smell that gave the house a just cleaned fragrance, a treat I reserved for Saturdays. If you were not careful your knees would be blackened and callused from the friction against the wood as you knelt. You had to use an old rag as a cushion.

~

I was in good shape back, unencumbered by the side effects of medication and a debilitating tiredness. Back then, and now what work I could find to do kept those awful thoughts at bay. Work was a source of joy. It was never a burden. It was my life, it was what I knew and it was my inheritance. It was the way of life in the country and all the mothers and grandmothers left back in our town on a workday was doing it. The guardian had his own life now; he started seeing someone in the district and that took his attention away from me. Good riddance!

If God had a plan for me I knew it not. He had started working His will in my life long before I recognized it. I graduated school before I was fifteen. Now my job was solely to take care of the house and occupy my time as productively as I could. I remember this because during this period my brother dying of cancer. He was sent home during my sixteenth birthday with loads of morphine and died five months later. Life went on abysmally and without hope because my champion had left me with no one to fend for me. There weren't any special days for cleaning or ironing any more, I did them whenever I felt like it.

The first time I heard the piano was on the lunchtime concert. I was alone, the children were at school, my dad was at work and my mom was in America. Our guardian/housekeeper no longer house kept, I did. It was my pride and joy to gather wild flowers and arrange them in a jar in the living room sitting just so on the dark mahogany coffee table. I would come indoors to admire the arrangement and sit on the cool yellow vinyl sofa in the darkened living room. It was then that I heard it. It came from the radio sandwiched between the sultry voice of the female disc jockey. It was a Tchaikovsky concerto something. I will never as long as I live forget the tingle that went up and down my spine. My body convulsed in rapture. That was my initiation to classical music.

I resolved to tune in everyday to the classical lunchtime concert and it was not difficult to find since there were only two stations. My chores were now scheduled around the concert. I would always contrive to be in the living room for my concert. I would dust and arrange and rearrange the furniture. I had long ago, learned that I had a gift for creating beautiful space.

~

I had even tested the theory by hiring a cabinet-maker to reposition our cupboards, cutting and sawing as I instructed. We painted the whole thing, cupboards and walls, with white gloss paint. I had a new kitchen and my dad was furious for a very short while. He never stayed angry for long. He forgave me because it was pretty.

I realize now that He had knocked at my heart's door and was seeking my recognition. He asked me to open it a crack. He walked me through asking for what I needed when I didn't know I needed it. "I will be with you always," He said. So he walked with me two miles to the library. The two miles seemed to go on forever while I moved forward, never looking back or sideways.

The lunchtime concerts had stirred my mind and I wanted to know more about this music. Where did it come from, what did classical mean. I had so many questions and I went seeking my answer. I didn't know where to look and I was too ashamed to ask. I realize I should have gone to the adult section not the children's as I did. So I ended up with a book on Ballet.

The book on beginning ballet had illustrations that showed you how to perform the moves. I decided that I would try the moves with the music. I reasoned that since I couldn't dance reggae, I had no rhythm, so what would be the difference if I failed.

At home I chopped the sleeves off a white mock turtleneck with golden metallic threads woven in stripes horizontally to create an outfit that looked almost like the one on the illustrated figure. I then cut the toes off an old sock to make my leg warmers. This outfit did not bode well in the sweltering heat of the tropics at midday.

~

I had found a new world of books and an ocean of discovery. I started dancing. It wasn't long before my bourgeoning, gawky, uncoordinated talent was discovered. That wasn't too difficult since I couldn't seem to stop. It was something new, something no one else knew about. I was often seen executing a plies and a leap. I am sure it looked more like two baby palm trees pressed down by a giant hand only to come bounding back up again. However it looked, I liked it.

The graceless high kicks that were my pride and joy bought me infamy when I fell on a pile of husked coconuts and cracked the shells of a couple. This little exhibition was a performance to showcase the advantage that books can give one even if one was not in school. None of us had a frame of reference for ballet since there were no televisions and the local movie house showed only westerns or karate movies.

The cracked coconut proved to be the demise of that little stint, but not of the books. I built a little library, again with partner in crime, the cabinetmaker, in an alcove to the right of the living room. The tiny four by four feet space seem perfect for shelves and a crudely constructed desk. It became my domain. With every cent I hoarded I bought books. Now I was a frequent visitor to the library and bookstore that doubled as the drugstore.

Several years earlier I had read the entire series of the Bobsy Twins mystery novels for teens, as well as the Hardy Boys and Nancy Drew mystery series. Then I had swept through several of the British romance novels known as Mills and Boone which were found in every bookshop, these you could finish in a day. I was already an established reader but now I need a challenge. I needed more, but what? I turned to textbooks and non fictions.

"I know the plans I have for you," He said. He must have, because I studied for and passed enough General Certificate of Examination subjects from the universities of London and Cambridge to make me feel good about my new self. My mind was alive even if my body was not in sync.

Amid the washing of dishes, I would have a book propped open on the sink. While sitting over a tub of dirty clothes and scrubbing them clean with carbolic soap I had a book open on the side. While cooking I would have a book open. I was reading to lose myself. I was reading so I couldn't think, but I didn't know I was walking in His steps.

Dinners became an adventure in the exotic. One night I decided to try the new flambé rec-

ipe I got from a library book. We had flambé
chicken that almost singed my father's nose
hair. As the grand finale we had a close house
fire with hollowed out, diced and refilled pine-
apple flambé. That night my brother and father
banned flambé. The grocer was instructed not
to sell me any more brandy.

From the basic provisions my father bought
we reaped the benefits of my newly acquired
knowledge. No two dinners were the same. The
cymbals clashed as I moved further and further
away from my pain. Even then, I wanted to
share my music, my song, though I didn't know
I had it.

I decided that we should have two rules.
One, we would only take the evening meal after we had washed and were seated together. If
one was missing I would keep dinner warm until they got home. Two, never, never investigate
what's cooking for dinner, don't open the pot
wait until it was served. My daddy kept breaking

both rules. The second one he dropped real fast when I flung the pot and its contents through the louvered window. I got a beating but he went without dinner and had to replace the panes of glass. His handkerchief never lifted the lids of my pots again. Sometimes his dinner was fed to our two dogs because he never came home.

We all learned to eat with knives and fork. I got a book on etiquette and painstakingly copied the placement for formal dining. Only problem was we didn't have some of the stuff. To this day my mom recounts the story as told to her, that I arrived at the supermarket with all my saving to shop for tableware. For the life of me I don't know why I was compelled to tell the Chinese shopkeeper that I was buying plastic because 'the children can't break these.' He looked from me to my brothers and sisters, he knew our family well, and his look asked if I was mad. He knew I was a year younger than my brother.

Had I kept my mouth shut he would not have given me that look and my brother and sisters would not have teased me mercilessly on the way back home. My embarrassment at buying plastic was short lived. It ended when I unpacked my beautiful new cream-colored melamine cups and saucers, the plates and glasses. We were off on a new adventure. That lasted awhile until the children rebelled. I had to relent with a few picnics on the ground and dinners on the vinyl sofa.

Chapter 5

The Song in the Silence

THE SHOFAR TRUMPET

Believe in yourself

"*T*herefore I tell you, whatever you ask for in prayer, believe that you have received it, and it will be yours." Mk. 11:24 (NIV). My mother was the one who started me on that path of discovery of my talents. She always gave me wonderful American things that fed my creative mind. A pink sewing machine that really worked, it looked like a lunch box when not in use. Crewel and embroidery sets were her choices for me not dolls. But long before those gifts when I was a tiny girl, about the time she had put me on my suitcase to wait for my dad, she gave me a tea set. It was a fifty-piece set that came in a box so big it seemed larger than me at the time. It was the best and biggest in the shop, I admired it and she bought it for me. My mom gave us lots of gifts. Every time she got mad at us and whipped us she gave us gifts and said she was sorry. We had more toys than all the other children in the village.

The tea set was what started us on the journey of fine dining. I think we were on a hunger strike way back then and the doctor told our mom to find creative ways to get us to eat. She had a carpenter build us a tiny picnic table with two benches. She placed our table and benches right alongside the family table and refilled our plastic teapot from the one on the dining table and replenishing our toy platter from her big serving plates. For a long time that's the only way we ate. I don't know where she got the patience from, but she did it. She indulged us and took delight in what amused us.

She too must have had cymbal moments, because at times she indulged us. I don't remember what happened to that table and its benches when we outgrew it. Now it was my turn to indulge my siblings. I made sure the kerosene lamp with its clear hurricane shade etched in frost with "Home Sweet Home" was cleaned and trimmed and ready for nightly homework sessions. While they did their work I would sit and crochet and supervised their progress. Many of the things I missed in school, because I skipped too many grades, I learned in those sessions. I went over their Latin with them. Logarithms, algebra trigonometry, religious studies and civics were subjects we mastered together.

When the lesson was too difficult and we didn't learn, I wrote a note of apology to the teacher, much to their consternation that a child was leading other children. My siblings did well, very well. They were good children. I made sure they were safe, fed and clean. As another ritual I would walk around checking the windows and doors. I would check under the beds and the shower and behind the doors. I don't know what I was looking for but I never found it. For that I am glad. They never got hurt on my shift.

We conversed in the Queen's English in our household, not all four of us agreed with this decision but it was a firmly planted rule to help with their studies. The Queen's English was the formal language of the island but it was seldom spoken around us. Outside the home we used a sort of Pidgin English, which is our country's pride and joy. A language we created from all the people who lived here and made it their land, including our African ancestors. But in order to pass a formal examination marked in the country of England, it's good to know formal English or the Queen's English. To achieve this end, years earlier I had taken to practicing from the BBC Newscast that was aired by short wave. By the time our island got to its own programming, I already spoke English with an accent. I spent many years trying to undo the way I pronounced my words. I have a Jamaican accent with British inflections, I tried to shake that accent, but it was too deeply entrenched.

~

During the years my brother Valdez was alive we were a complete family. It was he who first heard the Song. It was easy with him there because he had heard and recognized the music within long before I did. One day he came home from school dressed as handsomely as always in well pressed khakis, clutching a green book as one would a treasure. In this book he had inscribed, 'to Valdez from Valdez with lots of Love.' He had bought a King James Translation of the Bible. He read from that green book continuously. He was in form five (grade 12) and he was the head-boy at his school, that meant that next to the principal and teachers he was the next in authority. In this office of school hierarchy he was empowered to assign detentions and to discipline students. He had his hands full with sports and school. Yet he read from the green book.

Then one Friday he asked me to iron his best shirt and trousers, he had heard of a church a few miles up the road he wanted to check it out. The next morning, a Saturday, he looked nervous but he left for church. He stayed all day. I started packing him a lunch. He did that for a couple of weeks until I decided that it was time for us his sisters to join him in whatever he was doing. We were a family. I laid out clothes for my sisters and my brother made breakfast and packed a lunch and we went with him to church.

It wasn't our first time in a church. We had gone to a Baptist church when we were really young, just because my mom was sorry for the preacher who had no audience on Wednesdays. We lived directly across from the church and rectory. Because he had no congregation on wednesdays she sent us to keep him company. It was a sad affair, this black robed preacher lecturing four little kids, two of them sucking their thumbs, amid *Chitty-Chitty Bang-Bang* and *Dr. Seuss' Cat in the Hat*. The Library doubled as church. We would go some Sunday and on Wednesday nights. When there was a special occasion such as Easter and Christmas others came and we were the main attraction singing *Jesus Loves Me This I know*.

This though was different, we sat together in church and knelt together in prayer age fifteen, fourteen (me), twelve and ten. At lunchtime we ate together sharing with other outside on the rough church grounds or in the fellowship hall. We would clean up and pack our stuff for the walk back home but not before we went back inside for more services. These people were considerate of each other and of four little kids travelling together. They seemed deeply religious and we liked to hear them pray while the others were humming old hymns. We worshiped with them for two years. *Still I did not recognize the song.* One summer a crusade/ revival came to town under the big tent and Valdez wanted us to go. He was by now a baptized under the water member of his church. We four were always together, the younger ones had no say in the matter. I would spend Friday cooking and packing a 'great' feast for these outdoor meetings under the big tent. We were conscious that others were looking on to see our spread. This was where families came to show off their unfamiliar foods and superior fare. We had to have good food because people were all around our friends sometimes came by to share our meal. I was a good cook. Too bad the melamine plates were now showing their years. How we did not get salmonella poisoning is something I will never understand. Our food would be kept in the basket until after the worship service over a loud megaphone. Families would gather on the grass and share their meal. The producers of the crusade had huge blocks of ice wrapped in burlap and buried in the ground to keep from melting. They chipped off pieces and distributed it among the crowd. My brother would go get our portion while I dished up the food.

We always knew that our family looked odd. We were all the same size. Except my brother, he had started stretching out when he turned sixteen. We sat there on the grass pretending we were a complete family and it was then that I used to see the sadness in his eyes. I knew what it meant, because I felt it too. We prayed the girls were too young to realize that we were alone. I thought that whatever had given him his sweet spirit would rub off on me so I decided to get baptized under the big tent that summer. For a person of reticence it was an experience that I have not forgotten

I was dipped in the cool water, came up and realized my white dress revealed everything I was made of. That experience did not give me any peace. It was agony. But it would be worth it if we remained a family here and beyond. *Still I did not hear the song.* On Friday nights we would have rousing worship as we sang and prayed together. My mother was so impressed with our worship that we would record us. But first the house was prepared and polished to a sheen. Now the smell of cedar wood and clean floors permeated the air on Fridays. Valdez sang in a voice that couldn't quite make up its mind, I screeched and another sister sang alto and the other soprano. We were a motley crew, but we were together and safe.

~

With this church in the woods I had a wider audience for my cooking skills. The matriarchs of the church would rotate homes once a month to cook for the church social. I enjoyed having the ladies over at my place and they never excluded me because of my age. I was the 'mother' of my family. They taught me how to manage large amounts of food and shared counsel with me, not once were they condescending. They were humble country folks who loved God. If they knew my story they never said. I never asked.

Still I did not recognize when he said to me "for the son of Man has come to seek and to save that which was lost." Because He had sent them I learned from these ladies and they from me.

I now had a semblance of normalcy in my life, when I wasn't hiding in my house I was desperately trying to be like those around me. I was almost sixteen. The ladies at the church tried to help me so too did the ladies of the community. They took me with them when they went in a group to the river and taught me how to wash on the rocks. They showed me how to balance a pan of wet clothes on my head, and when it fell off they took me back to the river and rinsed them.

When I would not go with them they left sugarcane, bananas, mangoes apples and other treats on my doorsteps. I did not recognize that He was courting me. His words said, "My lover is mine and I am His; he browses among the lilies." In His gentle manner He was pulling me from my prison, using His light to cast out the shadows of shame. I was not the model the mothers of the village used to judge their daughters. I kept myself clean and I was described as industrious and virtuous. A misnomer if I ever heard one.

They had forgotten about my shame, I had not. I lived among them knowing they knew, and wondering when I will slipup so they could remind me. A razor's edge is an uncomfortable place to walk. If they didn't see me I couldn't be on the edge so I stayed away from people. I had no skills to lead the life they or their daughters led. I was different from others; I had been excavated for my treasure. I had no idea that my treasure was still intact because He had guarded it.

During the two years I watched my brother become a kinder more compassionate Christian I felt nothing; *I had not heard the song.* My brother's compassion would forever be underscored in my heart as the day I came home from the hospital.

It was before he became Christian that I saw it. The taxi had taken me home from the hospital and I was still reeling from the pain of expelling the replica. He had knelt at my bedside and wept for me. He was a boy, an innocent boy, but he knew what had happened. He did not speak of it; he simply held my hand as I watched the tears slide down his cheeks. I didn't cry; I was fascinated by the transparent brown of his eyes with its tiny flecks of gold. I had never seen anyone's eyes that close-up before. He had our mother's eyes. It made their appearance striking. He wept because of my shame and my pain while I stared blankly into his eyes. I don't think he had heard his music yet; it would be a year later that he became a Christian.

~

Three years from that day of holding my hand he died of Sarcoma. Cancer and his maker had claimed him. Before he went he left a legacy of bravery and strength that far surpassed his years. He died at the age of seventeen. He had discovered the lump in his leg after the soccer season and we would work on it with linseed oil. He was oiling his bat for the cricket season and knew that this was no time to be in pain. Each night I would make a poultice and apply a hot compress, but nothing worked. We all went to the doctor together. We did everything together. My mom always said we looked like soldiers all lined up in size order. My sisters sat in the waiting room while I went in with my brother. He examined him and told us he needed a biopsy and that we should call our mom. Our mom had set up accounts at the dentist and the doctor, we never needed money, and they sent the bills to her in America. He gave us coins for the pay phone and we used it to place a collect call. By the weekend our mom was home. I t was my brothers turn to go the endless rounds of doctors and to be cut open.

Before six months had passed, he had lost one of his legs. He was in and out of hospitals, yet his spirit remained sweet. When he could he would go to school, that would have been his graduating year. I don't remember what his ambition was, even if he had one, he tried not to be discontented. The amputation did not stop his music I realize that now. Even though he realized his body was dying he also knew it was well with his soul. He had heard it said to him, "Arise, go your way. Your faith has made you well."

He was never well in body again. He was in a hospital in Annatto Bay, way past the strawberry fields and the beaches to a room overlooking a veranda and with its own bathroom and a folding chair for my mother to sleep close to him. The narrow bed was propped up to support his head. Calling for us and asking the teachers and principal from his school to step outside a bit. We had interrupted singing and prayers. He bid us do for him for the last time. He bade us goodbye and extracted a promise to meet him in Heaven. With a resounding clang the cymbals clashed again because he had left with me his best wishes. He made sure I knew that God was not pleased with the treatment I had received up to that point on earth. He lamented the fact that I was invisible to my parents. My mom also heard and wept. He was saddened to leave me behind but was convinced that it was best that he suffer the pain. The morphine they sent home to keep him comfortable could not stop the phantom pains. Nothing could help him regain his internal organs eaten away by the cancer. He died of starvation. Still his music must have soared because he was compassionate to the last minute, asking that my mom be secretly sedated for that his last night on earth. For one last time it was just the four of us in that hospital room, as we said our goodbyes. Others were waiting, mother, father, teachers, and friends and family, yet it was just us as we fed him and combed his hair for the last time. He said he had no regrets because he knew he would have a chance to meet us again.

He was glad to go, sparing us, if he had a choice, but I was angry. Why couldn't it be me. I wanted to leave this earth also I needed it more as I was bad and he was good. What went wrong? I had no clue what he was talking about all I knew was that it should have been me that entered that sweet meadow filled with beautiful yellow flowers. It wasn't my time. I let him go. He went with his peace and compassion.

Somehow, church faded into the background. We stopped going after a while.

~

My father got me a job with the ministry of agriculture when I was seventeen. I took the bus to work and felt grown up. I had waited a long, long time for seventeen. Thirteen was far behind me and I was not as small as I used to be, people would take me seriously now. I will have a voice. I worked as a clerk in the bookkeeping office by day and attended accounting classes at night. I failed in both dismally.

I had also failed in secretarial classes at the catholic high school where I attended its extended day school. I would glare at my nemesis, the black Underwood typewriter with its rounded keys jutting out in an obscene grin. No matter how hard I tried, I couldn't get my fingers to conform to the commands of the brown-habited Nuns. Pitman and Gregg shorthand proved to be too elusive for me to grasp. My hand, eye, and brain refused to work in unison to get me a working at a speed of sixty words per minute, at the very least. They kicked me out when I could not advance past eighteen. That's how I ended up in night school.

"I know the plans I have for you," He said. He must have, because I sure didn't. I didn't fare much better at the Ministry of Agriculture. My job required a florid cursive handwriting, one I did not possess, to post entries in the gigantic journals. Reconciling a trial balance was far, far beyond the scope of my reach. I was horribly misplaced in this dusty darkened room with the tobacco-chewing old men, bent over from too many years of lugging the big books. I was graciously let go.

Left at loose ends with no job, no real working skills and still to young for much of anything, I turned to my books again. I examined various careers and decided that I should work with what I have, my cooking and cleaning skills. I was very good at those. I could do them with my eyes closed. I took myself off to the prestigious Home Economics school in Guy's Hill to train for something, I'm not sure what, but it must have been good because I really wanted to do it. I applied to the Headmistress for entrance and was refused. My letter of application had preceded me and I had arrived in a very large, very yellow Publics Works dump truck. My father was too busy but he remembered to send the truck. My sister accompanied me.

The woman took one look at me, the truck, my sister, the driver and no parent in attendance, sent me back home without granting me an audience. That was the end of that. I continued to dabble with my paints and make a general nuisance of myself. There was nothing else to fix in our house I had fixed everything so I went visiting the older ladies who were at home like myself. We would drink 'bush' tea that was kept on embers all day and watch them work. I had only two ladies that I regularly visited, the ones that didn't gossip. Most of the time we just sat in silence until it was time to go home. Back then I didn't talk much.

My dad must have felt sorry for me because when he bought a tiny kitten for my sister and for me he brought me a tutor. He was the son of one of his friends; the lad was going to art school in the city that year and my dad asked his friend to have his son help me with my drawings. The young man would come to the house after school since he was still in high school, and teach me perspective and proportions. He taught me how to find the plumb line and various art terms. He showed me how to use pastels and graphite.

I worked diligently on my homework assignments, sketching every piece of furniture in the house. As well as anyone who would pose for me; the two dogs, the cat and myself included. Because of his influence I applied to art school.

Since I had nothing better to do it seemed like a good idea. I was nineteen when my letter of application was accepted and I was granted an interview. My sister and I boarded a country bus in the swirling mist before dawn, which meant we had to walk two miles in the dark to get the bus. The big bus was laden down with market baskets of all sizes and shapes tied with the identifying color of its owner, crates of chicken and produce like bundles of sweet sugarcane and whole bunches of green bananas were tossed on the top. Every time we made a deep curve with a steep drop around junction Road, That ole country bus swayed dangerously from side to side around deep curves and gave all its riders a sense that at any minute the bus would slide down the gully. We made it to the city in one piece and got off the bus in Half-way-tree and found our way to the Cultural Training Center. Culture shock! It was a world strange and fascinating to us. Our shoes were caked with the mud from the inclement weather in the country and we must have looked like two country bumpkins straight of a tourist board commercial.

This time I was old enough to be without a parent. My interview went well and I was asked back to the entrance examination to prove my abilities in art of drawing. Our second trip to the city was less scary as we now knew where we were going and what to expect on the bus. My sister sat outside the examination room as I sketched from the still life during the morning session and a nude in the afternoon. I pretended that seeing a nude woman was no big deal! In reality I was shocked, nothing I had read had prepared me for this. While I was nervously trying to pass my examination, my sister was buying me a celebratory gift. I asked if it wasn't a bit premature to celebrate with the page green scarf. She was that confident I would get in. I did.

We later marveled at the difference in our appearance to those of the students we saw. Most of them were city kids; some had even come from nearby islands. Some drove their own cars and smoked cigarettes; they seemed so sophisticated to our naivety. I'm a quick study; I soon learned to smoke and to keep the mud from revealing my true identity. It never quite worked, as one professor insisted on calling me 'country girl.' By the time I was twenty I was almost citified, but not quite. I was still traveling on the country bus to and from school.

My mom used a family connection to get me room and board in the city. When they didn't pay boarding I started earning my keep by doing what I knew best, cleaning and cooking. Rather than pay what he owed, my dad had me pack my bags and moved me to a distant relative of his. We had skipped without paying. That galled, those were not my principles.

When he didn't contribute to my new household I was refused food and left sitting outside on the stoop to work by streetlight. I am not sure how long this continued, but it must have been long enough for my body to protest. It's a wonderful thing when you are not aware of your person, when you can operate without emotion or feeling. It leaves you oblivious to your condition and the wonderment of those around you. That little bit of Nirvana landed me in the hospital for two weeks.

I had been going to school day after day without food, working all night, so my body refused to go on until my mind listened. I didn't care about my body it had betrayed me too many times. I didn't need it and it sure didn't need me. Besides what could I do about the food situation, nothing. I wasn't about to beg, I'd what I got when I got it.

The official diagnosis was nervous breakdown, but I think it was the less glamorous starvation. My keeper wept that she had not treated me with more kindness. She apologized, swearing to do well by me but my mom took me away and never heeded her plea for a second chance. I'm not sure if they ever paid her.

This was my second brush with a mental institution. This time I stayed two weeks and attended daily sessions with a psychiatrist. I was in the very exclusive and clean St. Josephs Hospital. My mom later told me that I had asked to have her kept away from me. She said I had disclosed a hatred for her. That must have been the first time I spoke of the year I was thirteen. It was just before my thirteenth year that she brought her wild grown son to live with us. She dumped him on us. She dumped him on us when the police could not handle him and went to America. Yes, I hated her. Her absences I could deal with; her evil child I could not. She had helped him escape the law and so brought a lawless person into our home.

He was a troublemaker they had said, come and get him before he kills his grandmother. He beats her and robs from her. So my daddy allowed him to live with us, then they went about their business as usual. To this day I have flash-back memories that cause me to break out in cold sweat and bouts of depression. He would come and scoop me from my bed at nights to introduce me to his brand of music. There were no doors on our four bedrooms just curtains. There was nowhere to run, nowhere to hide. He would always find me, under the bed, against the wall but I could never escape him.

Why didn't I scream, why didn't I tell? That's why the judge later said it was my fault. I was a bad girl. Couldn't anyone see? Couldn't they hear? I guess not. Not until I started to swell with his ghastly replica did they come. They came outraged and angered. They came with po-lice and dragged me off to give statement after statement. Trying to get me to say it was some-one else. The police asked me if I like it, wanted to know what he wore each time he came and got me. I couldn't remember but still they ques-tioned me.

I wanted to die. I was so ashamed. No one would allow me to cry they kept saying shut up. I don't remember where my daddy was, he never came to me when the police came and got me. He wanted to stay out of it I guess. It was just the policeman and I; my mother was off someplace weeping about her bad luck. They never let me cry, I had to give the statement. Late in the night they took me back home and kept my brother. My mother didn't look at me and the other was kept away from my contamination. For the first time in my life I slept alone. The next morning started the questioning all over again.

It was one of my sisters who had written my mom with the new carryings on in our home. She came home took one look at the situation and ran screaming and hollering for all including the police to hear. She had a very dramatic faint at the station. That's when they came and got me. I knew what was happening to me, it had happened countless times before, only this time he never got tired of me. My mother knew this had happened before, her friends and now her family had their way with me, she never pressed charges before. She should have when I was two and four and all the other times. Why now this stink.

Yes I knew what was happening and I was ashamed.I tried running away and they always brought me back, what was I supposed to do. Now everyone is saying it's my own fault. The months that followed are sometimes lost to my memory only to return when I least expect it. I am not sure which is worst, the invasion of my body or the circus that was made of it with me being it's chief freak. Memories would come popping in my head and I can see it in vivid colors and taste the bitter gall of it. When it happens it is my music that brings me back on track. The music lays me down to rest, enfolds me in its notes and shelters me till the storm has passed.

The total number of days I lose to the memories are lessening each year. One memory could be of the police escorting me to the local clinic to be tested even though I was clearly enlarged. One police officer would stand guard at the door to the examination room while another went in with me to explain why we were there. All this time my mother would be hollering about her misfortune at having such a sluttish daughter. I would pretend not to see the other patients as they whispered and openly stared at me. You know something is up when the police escort a little girl to the doctor.

Another memory that plays itself over and over again is that of the final trial, I see myself mounting the endless stairs of the colonial style courthouse to a trial that was well publicized. A gawking, buzzing throng was hovering like vultures waiting for a juicy morsel. I have no memories of my father during this period. Someday I may ask him where he was. The magistrate pronounced her verdict, I should have known better, I should have told. He was free to go. He, my half-brother walked out of court a free man and I was sentenced to an eternal prison of shame and guilt.

"You judge according to the flesh; I judge no one. And yet if I do judge, my judgment is true; for I am not alone, but I *am* with the Father who sent me." These are His words and they comfort me. I was tried and condemned in the eyes of the world. All except my fourteen-year-old brother.

I survived those years by shutting down all thought and feelings. I pretended I couldn't see people and they couldn't see me. I went back to my village and was shown the newspaper that trumpeted my shame, and pretended that it did not exist. This must have been what was revealed during those two weeks in the hospital. I don't know, my only memory of the place is the taste of canned grapefruit juice and the kindly face of a doctor.

That trip to the hospital was occasioned by the further betrayal of my body. That same body that I had ignored had gotten itself all twisted. The right side refused to work and it stupidly contorted my face and right hand in the process of seeking my attention. I had no time for that in my first year at art school. My mom applied for and got me a leave of absence from the school. I'm not sure what she told them. We never discussed it.

I left St. Josephs Hospital, not as I had arrived but on my own two feet, nourished and coaxed back to life. "He restores my soul." He sure did. "For you are with me; your rod and your staff, they comfort me." I must have used His staff as my crutch to go back to school and complete my first years and the three others. "You anoint my head with oil; my cup runs over." I took the lodging situation in my own hand by running away to a farm one hundred miles from school. I traveled the busses through St. Andrew, Clarendon, Manchester to arrive in the savannah lands of St. Elizabeth.

The land was hill-less in most places and it was swaying with thigh high fluffy-top grass. It was astonishing to behold, miles and miles of this thing. I had not been in this parish since I was a little girl when we had taken the train to meet my mother's white haired and blue eyed family. St. Elizabeth was filled with lots of people like that. I had come to live with my big sister, only she didn't know what was moseying up the lane to her house with the big watermelon patch. This kind and loving sister was my mother's first born. She was one of two children my mother had before she met and fell in love with my father. The land she owned was the one from witch my half-brother was ejected to land a place in our home. Everything was big here. My sister let me stay awhile and pretty soon I was in touch with a friend from school, and she had her family invite me to live with them. Her dad paid my tuition and he gave me lunch money. He even drove me to school along with his daughter.

I left their home to my own after I landed a great job in a fabulously modern design studio. All my wonderful new talents and some of the old ones served me well in this job. It was a success and I loved working with the studio owner whose name was also the name of the studio. He was also chief designer. His audacity paid off because the jobs were pouring in. This job lasted through art school and so it comfortably situated me.

Whether before or after working for the country's top advertising agency upon graduation I worked as a _marker maker_. A marker Maker's job was to fit patterns on a thick precise stream of tourist shirt fabric for optimum usage and reduction of scrap fabric. One would fit and mark around the patterns on a giant sheet of brown industrial paper so that the marked sheet would become the guide for the pattern cutter with his giant saw/cutter. It was pleasing to see your work coming off the production line as finished products.

In my senior year before I graduated, I was courted by a well known New York Art School and one of the leading advertising agencies on the island. The advertising agency won me. My job at the advertising agency was another adventure. All was categorized as an adventure. Nothing was connected and a part of the process of learning. I wasn't sure how long my good fortune would last. The adventure continued at this very large agency. Three men with lots of power formed the agency and employer lots of talented people to handle the the many consecutive projects. It was a dream come true to be asked to write copy for radio and television. I wrote advertising copy by nights in my apartment and completed them into storyboard by day. Only problem was I was told *"Your spelling is atrocious."* They tested me in several areas of the business, I was sent on a soda pop shoot. I was a major shoot for a very large export company. Occasionally I would meet with a client to pitch my ideas and at times I was simply allowed to sit in as part of the creative team. Being able to sit in on client meetings to brainstorm was a privilege I will never forget. I was even asked to illustrate an article for the country's inflight magazine. I enjoyed this job until one day I picked up my purse and left the job. I am not sure what caused me to do so but in under a year it was over.

How I kept that job is beyond my comprehension. I quit when it interfered with my drinking. They could smell the stuff coming through my pores anyway so whom was I kidding. I know they had my ticket because the secretary once told me I reeked. They knew what I would drink, Johnny walker Black when we went on shoots. The bar stool was my perch. Still I never looked back or sideways. I did my job and drank. I didn't know it then but I was self medicating and reeling from people contact in my new life, wondering if they knew.

~

Walking off that job I walked into my own sub-contracting business. Things were happening so rapidly that I just went with the momentum. Before I knew it the business was growing. I had all kinds of clients. Hotels, travel agencies, import export business, insurance companies and individuals all purchasing monogrammed sets of leather bound note pads to thank their clients for their business.

I had my first national and international exposure in my final year in art school. One year after I left school I was honored for my work as an entrepreneur with a start up business that was doing well. The honor of being invited to join in a national expose of *Women in Business* fed my belief that I could stay hidden in the backgrounds only to emerge when absolutely necessary.

In the midst of all this, my dad came for a weekend visit and stayed two years. I was finishing my last two years of college. I had my own flat, a little cottage, and he simply moved into my one bedroom flat with me. He did so in increments. I was glad for the company of my father and seized the opportunity to get to know him better. It turned out that the government had taken him out of retirement to fix a troublesome road in the big city one that was having drainage problems and so caused floods. I was proud of my old fashioned dad and his skills.

Graduation was to last three days and I hadn't invited anyone. My mom flew in from America anyway for the occasion. I had not invited them because my high school graduation was treated as just another day to them. No one went with me. I had waited for them and when they showed no sign of interest I took the twenty-mile ride by bus and got there late. I sat in the back pew of the huge Anglican Church that the school had rented. The Church was located on Main Street across from the courthouse where I had been a litigant in circuit court a few years earlier. I watched my classmates who were all older than me by at least two years, some by four, as they sang and glowed from the choir loft. I did not care for a repeat of that for my college graduation.

My mom had bought me an answering machine as a graduation gift. I was so stoned from ganja that I do not remember much of the week-long affair. Graduation from the region's only art school is a grand affair with many dignitaries attending But I can't remember all who visited my booth.

I knew my show was a success because visitors kept coming and would linger long in my booth. I could not savor my success because I was too frightened. I thought if they only knew what a fake I was, if they saw the hollowed out shell they would know that my beautiful work was a fluke. But I did not want them to see beyond the outer shell that was at its human peak of form so I hid behind a stoned, glazed stare and the black lacquered nails that echoed my rebellion. I could not escape His plans for me. I could not escape the strength with which He had imbued me.

He continued to rectify the misdeeds of my earlier life and continued my education of self worth. He kept me going telling me I could do it. I did it so often I started to believe it. Success after success followed me. But still I didn't believe in Him. I didn't know him. He widened my horizons and sent me on photo shoots for ads I had helped to write. He allowed my copy to be aired in a radio commercial. He sent me as guest speaker to an elementary school, all the time offering his staff as support. I didn't know it then.

When I started my own business he encouraged me and found me clients of insurance agencies, hotels and travel agencies. I was twenty-five years old. The success was too much, too soon. I was still just filling my days and it was becoming more than I wanted or could handle. So he gave me a way out. I worked on my business part-time while working as a product coordinator for the government. I could help others get a kick-start to their business. I was good at that. I was full of ideas; I was new to the peopled world, so I had not yet learned my limitations. I believed anything was possible and that philosophy usually proved true.

Through my entrepreneurship I was brought to the attention of the manager of the cottage craft organization. There I worked closely with an agent of the United Nations Development Agency to improve cottage craft skills under my portfolio. Skilled artisans were bought into the country to work on designs we conceptualized then trained others and those other trained another group and so on. When I got an idea to promote the cottage craft industry on the national aircraft carrier, I got the go ahead and organized one of the largest craft fairs ever. Nothing stopped me. "You can do all things through Christ who strengthens you." He had been carrying me for a long time but I did not know He was there, so he got my attention. He asked for me to open the door wider and face Him. I didn't and He didn't quit.

It was a Friday night, I asked my father to go visit in the country, as I needed the apartment to myself. Through all my apparent success I was drinking heavily and smoking just as hard. I would have Amaretto de Sonora for breakfast and Johnny Walker Black for dinner with pretty little in between. I was traveling the country in my boss's car with her driver, living the good life but I hated it. I was disgusted with myself and wanted nothing to do with the empty person that I was. With my dad gone I cleaned my flat and gathered all the drugs I had been hoarding for this moment. I got my pillow and put the radio on and then got the final implement; the shiny new Gillette razor blade I had taken from my dad's shaving kit.

With the black rotary phone in the closet under the rest of the pillows and the answering machine turned off. I was at peace. The moment I had been waiting for had arrived. I must have laughed out loud in my pleasure. My beautiful yellow meadow awaited me. I would walk among the yellow-topped flowers and roll in the grass like I did as a little girl in Castleton Gardens. Then I did it. Now it would be over. It wasn't.

I awoke to the sound of banging on my shuttered window. It was my landlady with a friend. "It's Monday morning;" they were saying, "have you slept all weekend? You didn't go with the driver when he came for you." I ignored their clamor and went straight to the green book. I knew somehow He had something to do with this failure. I had this burning desire to read Job 6: 8 "Oh, that I might have my request, that God would Grant me the thing that I long for! That it would please God to crush me, that he would loose his hand and cut me off!" I shelved my amazement and the implication of those words and answered the door. A public service announcement had been sent out earlier by radio requesting family or friends to come see about me. My family was once again on the way to see what mess I had created this time.

So began my third trip to the hospital. The island had three mental health facilities and I had visited all three. My wounds were dressed on an outpatient basis. I was not admitted, courtesy of my family's connections because that would have involved the police, so I was mandated to attend weekly sessions at the clinic. Once a week I joined my cohorts with the glazed eyes and slack jaw. During the day I wore two very large copper bracelets made especially for me. If anyone guessed at the reason for the bandages beneath the bracelets they never said anything.

I continued with my work since there was no way to get off the ride of life. Once you are on you stay on until He takes you off "everything under heaven is mine," He said in Job 41: 11. Those texts I knew because I had looked it up that Monday morning. It was at this point in my life that things escalated to a giant change, life as I knew it would change yet again. My mom suggested a change of residence and invited me to live with her in America. I came. Before I left my dad surprised me with his care and concern for me. He proved that he knew me well so he shared this bit of insight with me, Through colloquial slang he said, "yuh don' trust nuh one. Yuh hav' the ways of the crab, always walkin' sideways.So nuhbody kno' yuh name. Is as if yuh ded." He was suggesting that I should use this opportunity to change and open my heart to people. My dad was simply saying I was walking through life avoiding all encounters. Sort of like walking through the raindrops without getting wet. Knowing it and acknowledging that my father knew me well was not something I could fathom until years later.

Chapter 6

The Song in the Silence

THE ORGAN YEARS

Graduate School

"My Grace is sufficient for you, for my strength is made perfect in weakness." 2 Cor. 12:7-10 (NIV). So began the Organ years. My flight circled and landed at JFK on February 22 after dusk. From my window seat I beheld the lights of New York. Never in my wildest dreams could I have imagined anything like it. From the sky it appeared to be bolts of black velvet strewn with bright white diamonds. From that height you could not make out individual buildings. Each shift and motion of the craft caused it to reveal another pattern of lights. As the craft descended lower eventually we were able to make out buildings. Buildings as high as the sky. Why on earth anyone would want to live in something like that? People and cars looked like toys. Having left the island late afternoon on ascent the view was that of neatly organized farm land and water for as far as the eyes could see with an occasional smattering of buildings and towns. The creative display of God's handy work was right there to see as he painted on canvas earth with pthalo-green, blue-green, emerald-green and yellow-green. Interspersed throughout patches of raw umber, that deep reddish-brown color of the land colored by bauxite, with its soil tilled into even corn-rows. That was nature as I was familiar with it, but this was different. This was the *Jewel of the Nile* and excess at its most bountiful.

After unpacking our bags we were taken to a restaurant on the water's edge. We were seated in a room made of glass on three sides and above. Sort of like sitting in a glass box on the water's edge. It was dark and the restaurant was lit with myriads of tiny white lights sparkling off the glass and white table linen. We were cosy with all the light and the chatter of my family who had booked this location to celebrate my arrival. It turned out the others were just as reflective as I was in the journey that brought me here; the reasons and events that led to this country and the promise of a new life. Suddenly I saw a tiny pinpoint of light dancing towards me, followed by another and yet another. This dancing chorus came straight in from afar within a few seconds the rest of their troops joined from all sides. Now were coming fast and furious seemingly to shatter the glass of the building but they didn't land a blow. I interrupted the others and asked what was going on. With glee they informed me *"that my dear was SNOW."* Everything was ordered perfectly for me to witness this miracle.

I arrived to glorious anonymity, lost in the bustling throng of New York City where I sought work. First I had to get used to the subway. After significant amount of time riding on the D train underground I decided to take the 2 train to see a different part of the city. I could hardly contain my scream at the burnt out buildings hastily shuttered up with plywood and covered with very large handwriting that made no sense. It was a while before I found out the history of that pace. I could not believe that people could be so displaced nor could I believe that I was viewing the America that I saw from the skies.

I picked up odd jobs that were a blessed relief in their mindlessness; there was no chance of success and I loved it. There was no need to escape the past by proving my worth. No one knew me, and no one cared. I was free to be nothing again. Nothing was my long time friend and I embraced her.

Pretty soon I got tired of all that nothingness and so I I applied for and was accepted and started a graduate degree. I love learning. The walks about the grounds looking at the historic buildings, the library stacks with clear glass brick floor, going to school on a part time basis and pitting my philosophy against others. This was all part of the world of academia and I loved it. I preferred theories to finger on keyboard creating computer designs. I was working frantically and enjoying myself that when my pigskin arrived in the mail I had no idea what to do with it. If you don't attend your graduation they send your degree to you in the mail. I am not good at attending graduations. Anyway using it was not in the plans it was a time filler and a pleasure. It was not a means to an end it was simply the means of escaping from myself. It was the means by which I escaped my pain and fear of withering to nothingness.

Learning seemed easy for me because I threw myself into it with fierce dedication and competition, getting lost in a book or project was always my escape. What I didn't learn, was how to stay in the peopled world. Graduate school made me realize that. I had gotten through art school with what was termed a nervous breakdown from a suddenly peopled world. I had left my comfort zone of hiding in my house to attending the only cultural training center in the Caribbean at the time. It housed the school of dance, music, art and drama. It was a lot of people milling about yet every class was intense. We were all vying for the top grade. In such an atmosphere of high completion, I thrived and did well for myself..

During art school I was introduced to drugs, which took care of the fear and pain for the rest of the days in school. I had quit drugs before I came to New York, trying to silence the noise in my head and heart. In fact I just got up and quit one morning. What was the sense in destroying yourself if God would not allow it? I was sober and conscious all through graduate school. Odd jobs paid for my education and board. I graduated from one of the City's top graduate schools with very good grades, but had failed miserably at interpersonal relationships.

Professors and colleagues alike tried to befriend me and offered their professional guidance to help me break into the design business here in America. I rejected them all. My thesis advisor encouraged me to publish my thesis but I didn't take her advice. I was offered graduate assistantships, which would get me in the mix on campus, I ran from all suggestion of involvement. My flashback episodes were getting more frequent and were lasting longer, sometimes for weeks. I was out of control. Through all this He kept waiting at the door where I had left Him, waiting for my invitation to enter.

Journal entry - July 5, 1997. "Today while driving home from church, it came to me quite clearly; it would be in my best interest to simply wait on the Lord for direction in my life. It will do absolutely no good to get anxious about my situation. If it is the Lord's will I will gather my thought and find direction and peace. I do need to take to the Lord the matter of feeling left out of things at church.

There was a time when I was difficult to be around. I think that time has recycled again. I find that I have very few friends and that situations seem only to worsen. I am not invited out with the gang any more. I feel so left out and lonely, but I am aware that there must be a reason for this. I believe the fault is within me. I need to correct it. Today, however, I was able to sit quietly and pray about my anger and frustration. The Lord resolved the matter right there and then. If only I would call upon the source to achieve this result more often. May God continue to work out his will in me and alleviate this feeling of abandonment."

The role of good nutrition

"...I will restore your health and heal your wounds, declares the Lord, because you are called and outcast, Zion for whom no one cares." Jer. 30:17 (NIV). Journal entry – October 4, 1997.

"I have spent the past three days by myself since church on Wednesday. I have holed up in a contemplative state that is not quite the same as a depression. I realize I must do something to stop the cycle of feeling rotten. This feels good as if I am doing something for myself. I have started a diet and cleansing regime. I've had many diets but this doesn't feel the same. I feel as if I really want this, I want my mind and body clear. I need to be. It will make me feel more in control. I also need to clear my body of impurities."

~

There are several approaches to wellness including holistic therapy, either by an herbalist or doctor of medicine, there is the traditional psychotherapy and psychiatrist combination, peer counseling, psychoanalysis, psychodynamic therapy, interpersonal therapy, cognitive therapy, behavioral therapy and brief therapies. Support groups are also another option, these groups follow the format of a "12-step" model. I had at some point or another employed varing combinations of these models. I always knew that if I am in good health I would feel better physically and spiritually.

~

I realized that I was in the best position to know how I felt so therefore I must make the first move to bring my body into balance. You see I was sick and tired of being sick and tired. I realized that wellness and learning about nutrition means becoming an advocate for yourself. Becoming an advocate gives you back your dignity and places choices in your hands. It allows you to gather information, attend advocacy meetings so you learn to ask for what you need. I learned to ask for a nutritionist with whom I kept a food diary after I told her what I would like to achieve.

~

For me advocacy dispelled isolation and provided a forum for understanding my symptoms and dispelled the feeling of being unwell. I came to this knowledge of advocacy after I was hospitalized one too many time. I did not agree with everything my doctors had to say or where they placed me. I did not want to get lost in a system and become a diagnosis. I was a child of God and that made me special, in my diet, what I heard and saw and how I was treated.

Chapter 7

The Song in the Silence

THE BELLS

Use your faith

"I give them eternal life, And they shall never perish; no one can snatch them out of my hand." Jn. 10:28(NIV). "Now I see through a glass darkly." His words said. And I did see darkly. I knew He was there but I did not know him. It wasn't until one night a friend and I were standing on the piers in Manhattan, gazing up into the night sky when he asked me about my belief in and knowledge of God that I realized that He would not wait much longer. I went back to my brother's green Bible to find out more about the God I believed in. I was now twenty-nine, yet He had waited all those years for me.

~

I recognized him as the One who gave me those promises. He reclaimed me as his rightful heir and taught me to appreciate his handiwork. I spent months studying the Bible and worshiping at home until one day my sister visited and enquired if I couldn't find a group of people who believed the same thing I did. "You are fearfully and wonderfully made," He said. I started looking at what He saw. I saw a woman. A person. I saw an attractive and smart person.

Over the years He has worked with me to open my heart to love and be loved. He held my hands when I cried with the first blossoming of femininity. He shepherded me through the agony of giving my heart in learning to love unselfishly as He had done with me. He showed me with tenderness and compassion, a glimmer of His love, because He knew I could never comprehend it.

Here in New York, miles away from where he started courting me, He bought me into His church and surrounded me with His people. People just like my brother. They believe the same things he had and worship on the same day as he had done. There was a wonderful bonus as the Lord further proved how thoroughly he restores you. The church I found in the telephone directory was a Hebrew Adventist Church. It was here that I learned about my heritage and studied the gospels with a wonderful teacher. If I were asked how I can be sure God loves me and cares for me I would say because of how he has treated me in the past. I am beginning to recognize it more frequently these days.

~

When I questioned where He was during my journey, He reminded me that "Yea, though I walk through the valley of the shadow of death, I will fear no evil; for you *are* with me; your rod and your staff, they comfort me." He reminded me that He was always with me, keeping at bay the one who sought to destroy me. I feel safe now, I know that whatever befalls He is able to take care of me.

~

Through His words in the Green Book, the Bible, I learned that He desired more for me, starting with peace. ' "For I know the plans I have for you," declares the LORD, "plans to prosper (Shalom) you and not harm you, plans to give you hope and a future. Then you will call upon me and come and pray to me, and I will listen to you. You will seek me and find me when you seek me with all your heart. I will be found by you," declares the LORD, "and will bring you back from captivity."'

The year 1996 proved to be one of the most difficult in my life. I had to make some serious decisions. I had managed to make a mess of quite a few things. I was facing some major issues with my perception of my lack of education. I had tried not to face them yet in face of my realization I went ahead and re-registered for my final year in graduate school. It was one of the most difficult things I had ever done. I was scared I would not live up to the school's expectation of me.

At that point I felt that academia was not for me, I had been using it as space filler because I did not know what to expect from one moment to the next. I recognized that moment was a very expensive panacea.

He bought me back from captivity. He is teaching me how to unravel the coils of slavery that was placed around me. My body and mind will always bear the scars of the battle, but my soul and my hope are eternally bound to Christ. That's when I heard the silence. His promise was kept. He silenced the voices of shame and condemnation. He took away the child that was a victim and replaced her with a woman that had walked the path with Him to victory. It was His victory over a foe that He fought viciously for me.

It was in 1996 that I finally accepted just how immature and unprepared I was for life. It is life itself that overwhelms me, not the individual situations as I had previously thought. When I find myself spending two days in bed hiding from my pain and responsibilities, I realize it's more than just depression; it is hiding from reality. At that point I wish I were someone other than me. I don't really see my self as a victim, I see myself more as a casualty. For so long I had lived in a bombed-out shell that I didn't know how to emerge out of.

I thought I had successfully hidden myself. Not because of the incest and its attendant trauma, but because I wanted to be a little girl. I wanted to be taken care of, never to feel pain, disappointments or disillusions. Somehow I figured that a life of ups and downs could be avoided if you lived in a safe cocoon. At the age of thirty-five it was no longer possible to stay in that cocoon so I tried some grown up projects. I bought a car and learned to drive, worked on relationships

Now all the instruments I had heard through the years have come together in a beautiful symphony orchestra. But it's not over; I know the final symphony has not yet been heard. I know the battle for my soul is still raging, but it's not my battle; it's His. He says He has one more promise to keep, that He will take me to a place where I will never know sorrow again. Where

I will never weep again. Where another child will never again be excavated to rob her of His sweet song.

I believe because He has kept His other promises. My flashback episodes are diminishing with each step I take with Him. But I understand its OK to proudly bear the scars of battle. A battle He fought on my behalf. He came in scooped me up and bought me to safety. He will nurse me back to life. Life eternal. He said "I go to prepare a place for you. And if I go and prepare a place for you, I will come again and receive you to Myself; that where I am, there you may be also. And where I go you know, and the way you know." "I am the way the truth and the life." He said.

In that Day my ungainly, faltering steps will be coordinated with the sweet, sweet symphony in a glorious dance with countless others who have listened to His song. I hear the music not just in my heart but also in my church where we sing and worship. My friends play beautiful music for all of us who have walked with Him to victory. Now I belong, I am the same as they are inside and out, because we belong to the same God. I will see my brother again on That Day and I will tell him he was right. It is OK more than OK; it was made right.

Chapter 8

The Song in the Silence

DRUMMING

Letting go

"Who comforts us in all our troubles, so that we can comfort those in any trouble with the comfort we ourselves have received from God." 2 Cor.1:4 (NIV). Just when I thought it was over, I got news that it wasn't over yet. I was diagnosed with bipolar disorder. The former term for it is "manic-depressive syndrome." In a sense the diagnosis was both a relief and a scare. I was frightened to find out that I had been living on the very edge of madness for a long time. A astounding madness, but I also found that those rare moments when you feel brilliantly creative. It was the creative highs that had propelled me out of my lethargic state of depression when I thought life was meaningless. It shrouded me with its brilliant light of creativity seeming to give me verve for life. That creativity also extolled its lot by bringing along chaos, a jumble of thoughts and rapid-fire speech. One friend termed it as my "headline-speaking phase."

During those moments I felt like I could conquer the world. I would come up with brilliant ideas for new businesses and other innovative ideas for the church's food pantry, grad-school projects and home decorating. They indelibly marked the passage, the ebbs and flows of my illness. A manic high is not long sustained, with this illness it is occasioned by a deep dark depressive state. During this time I feel as if I am constantly chasing my tail. How can I live up to the pace I had set during my manic state? How could I execute the seemingly great ideas I had conceived? How can I keep others from guessing that something was wrong? As you can imagine, it was a torture to keep up with myself and with the travesty.

Mania also extracts another price of feeling so good that you need very little sleep to sustain it. I remember going for two years on two to three hours of sleep. I t was during my graduate years. I was working in a prominent hotel as a room service order-taker. I would arrive for work at eleven o'clock and clock-out at seven in the morning. I would hop on the subway and arrive home at eight to start my school day. I would make breakfast and chat with my mom and sister, then fall into bed until ten or eleven depending on the time of my class. I was a full time student at Pratt Institute. Sometimes my classes would begin at twelve at other times they would begin at two or three.

There were days when I would try to cram a museum or gallery visit before class or simply drop off and pick up my work at various production agencies. I was also researching my thesis so my days were well spent. After classes in Brooklyn, I would take the train to Manhattan and start the rounds all over again. On days when I felt I was stretching It, I would take in a movie in Times Square before heading over the Grand Hyatt for my night shift. If there were early staff meetings I had to make those also.

When I wasn't in mania I could hardly keep up with this pace. Every graduate student knows how frantic the pace of school and work can be, but when you are suffering from this illness you think up the most grandiose projects that would require enormous energies to execute. If you are required to write a simple paper you write a trilogy. If you are required to create one painting you create a triptych. Everything had to be bigger and better. The manic state also brings the noise. The racing thoughts and quicksilver response to stimulus plus an intense connection with everything around you are also part of this illness. You feel more sharply every nuance of every painting and every lecture. Every slight becomes a catastrophic rejection. The slightest sign of acceptance becomes the declaration of love. That is what the mania feels like.

On its heels the depression brings the long black spells of nothingness. It was during the nothingness that I often thought of death. Death was never far from my thoughts. It accompanied me for almost every waking moment and during my sleep the thoughts would intrude in the form of dreams. In my dreams its crocked finger would beckon me in a seductive manner. "Come on take the plunge, or are you chicken," it would seem to say. My song kept it at bay and I know I am very fortunate because the death rate from the illness is very high indeed.

Yeah, I have been through my suicide moments, ever since the time I had slit both my wrists open I was never again tempted beyond what I could bear. He had made a promise to me and He kept it. I would think of plunging the sixteen floors from my beautiful apartment, but I never did. I would think of swallowing all of my medication but I never did. While cooking or peeling a fruit the knife would often beckon with a bewitching sorcery, but it never enticed me beyond my endurance. The car I was blessed with offered its siren song, seducing me towards a light pole or an outcrop of huge rocks, but I had the master with me at the wheel, so I would ride on by.

Yeah, death beckoned me all right, but "stronger is He that is within than he that is without." I was always conscious that I could not live up to the frantic pace I set in my manic phase and it defeated me many times. In the classroom as a student I would dominate the class with raising my hand to almost every question proffered by the teacher. I also had profound queries that were often beyond the scope of answering in the class. I would often be conscious that I was too much and would duck out of class as soon as I could. My hasty exit was made to cover my shame. I was always embarrassed about one thing or another. During the manic phase it seem as if I am driven by some need to know, to take risks to be all that I can be and more. I want all that life can offer and I want it at that moment. I see the world as bigger and broader than I am and the realm in which I live and I want to explore it and all the possibilities it offers.

The episodes come with an exhilarating clarity of mind and a profound grasp of concepts. I would quickly process what the lecturer was hammering at and counter with a seemingly brilliant question or comment. When I wasn't manic I couldn't understand why the accents and concepts seem to elude my understanding. I took to taping my required reading and play them over and over until I got it. I would read and take copious notes. To the onlooker I must have appeared quite intense and studious at my work. Within I was petrified. Is it any wonder that I loved my manic highs?

After the manias comes the somnolence. Following that is the blackness that would spread its heavy cloak of doom and despair around me. There were days when I got up thinking that living should be the easiest thing in the world to do, but everything seemed so drab as if painted by a muddy finger that was none too talented. I should have marveled at the fact that I can hear birds sing in this part of the city, but I wished they would cease their heralding of this new day, one I did not ask for. Those were the days that I walked through as if dead. Everything inside is empty, flat there is no feeling, there is no place in me but blackness. I would swing my legs off the bed in that instinctive motion of walking, one that seems to have nothing to do with my brain, nothing to do with who I am because I cease to exist.

Journal entry – July 28, 1997. " I do not know how to proceed. I only know I want to be out of this state of limbo. I now desire more from my life. I am tired of this sort of life. It seem I do not know who I am. I am not being a good friend to my girlfriends. I am not contented with my life. I don't know if I am coming or going. Church does not mean much to me right now. I have practically no spiritual life. I want to recapture that. I need a re-conversion experience. Maybe I should attend some sort of tent meeting. I took some sleeping pills yet still I cannot sleep.

I now live with the understanding that those of my age group seem not to understand me. My highs and lows coupled with a generous heaping of the child I never was, and is putting back together, can be confusing to those taking a glancing at the surface and who are believers in the sanctity of first impressions. The paradox is that the older folks find me exciting and interesting. As the Lord uncovers within me goodness, honesty and love I will be able to tolerate other as they try the same with me. I am sharing this, my life with you so you may take heart and comfort in my education which is life's lessons.

"What is education?" I suppose our first thought would be that of the journey from kindergarten to graduate school and beyond. For some of us, education is what we painfully sit through in a classroom or workshop in order to land a job. While, on a higher plane, we all like to think that spiritual education occurs by just a quick reading of the Bible. I am here to share with you that education is much more than what we take for granted.

There are many charts, graphs and pyramids that tell us how to rate education. But education's purpose is... redemption. Ultimately it's your future beyond the grave that should be secured by pointing to Christ. Here, today, *in the natural as some say*, Education, *redemption that is*, is what we need so you can tell the Boss I get it! Redemption is what the child/student shows when he or she passes the state tests. In this case what is redemption? Years of your parents' hard earned money as they pay for you to do your job during your career as a young student. It is a job, not just killing time until you are grown. In the case of formal schooling for me I am afraid I took the outcome lightly.

It is said; *you can give a man a fish and feed him for a day*, but teach a man to fish, and you will feed him for a lifetime. If fishing isn't your thing, then how about horse farming? What I am saying her is that it does not matter what you trial is, learn from it. There would be no point in writing this book if I did not share my thought and beliefs with you. Some have remained silently hidden in my head all this time. Now that I have your attention I will share it and hope you understand. The saying goes, you can lead a horse to water but you can't make him drink. All the lectures, slide shows and field trips in the world won't hammer education into your head. Gathering bits and pieces of information does not guarantee that you have achieved education.

What is needed is an understanding of the fact that "education is what survives, when what we learnt, is forgotten". These words of B.F. Skinner points to the fact that you may get the right answers on your third grade math homework but miss the concept during the follow up topic the next day. Mind you, education is not something that should be used to boast about. Paul in 2nd Cor 11:16-21 spoke of the foolishness of parading your credentials. We could take a lesson from him in figuring out the old adage that *"some people go to school to get a degree and some people go to school to get an education."*

A point I would like to make is that of the outcome of two men who never finished grade school. Thomas Edison the inventor of the light bulb and Henry Ford who gave us cars. They succeeded because they knew how to research, collect information for a selected project and process knowledge. All I know is that what comes out of me is what I know to do and say, I trust that fierce urging in me that says give of your life to this cause. ... I will give you beauty for ashes.

Those who already have the Light of the world know what I am talking about. I Cheryl find it no good to reading through the bible in a year without understanding context, purpose, or knowledge of the people and customs. It serves no purpose for me *other than a time consuming task.* I hope the book is not that. It's not a volume of salacious stories to embarrass people. It is a labor of love sharing a journey into peace from turmoil.

Remember the purpose given to education? Redemption! As a teacher and a student of life and the scriptures, I will share with you that the best method of education is to teach what you learn. I share my testimonies with you to give you strength. I am also sharing some adorable little texts I learned, my setbacks and my hopes, in doing this I would have fulfilled God's call to education; that God offers comfort to all. 2 Cor. 1:2-8

Chapter 9

The Song in the Silence

THE TEMPLE CHOIR

God and His healing touch

"*B*ut I will return you to health and heal your wounds,' declares the Lord, 'because you are called an outcast, Zion for whom no one cares.'" Jer.30:17 (NIV). During the times I am showing symptoms of bi-polar or experiencing the flashback of post traumatic stress, all I can think of is that there is nothing to live for, there are no yesterdays and there will be no tomorrow. I think that life is a cruel joke where you are left in limbo, with breath but nothing to breath it into, with life but not thriving, and with a voice but no one with which you want to speak, and no song in your heart.

Death seems like it' just around the corner, within my grasp, but it's not yours to administer, having tried it and snatched back to life. The Lord lets you know that it will not be so if it is not allowed. Hate is far from your grasp; you can't hate your life if you don't have one. The days don't seem long because there is no awareness of time; it's just the motions that carry you through. The nights are no different other than that it is a dark shroud cloaking the blackness within you. It's a place where you scream in silence as in the painting by the renowned artist Edvard Munch; he must have understood this when he painted *The Scream* in 1893.

The blackness would spread its heavy cloak of doom and despair around me but I could not be penetrated. The light of Him who guides me would infiltrate the seemingly indomitable blackness and bring me into the knowledge of His love and presence in my life. Time and again He would sing His sweet song to me through the words of the Bible. *"...Now I know in part; then I shall know fully, even as I am fully known"* 1Cor. 13:12 (NIV).

I now understand that I did not really perceive, but now with medication supervised by a skilled psychiatrist and regular visits to licensed psychotherapist, I have a chance. My song conquered the cacophonous noisiness of the beckoning gloom in the silence. I used to think the words of the scripture referred to in the above paragraph pertained only to an epoch such as the beyond, the New World after this life. Now I know that those words can also refer to an awakening of the mind and soul such as mine. I answered God's call to freely come, and I found me. Myself infused with the Light in me. For so long I had been a stranger dwelling within my skin, now I am free. I await further revelations as I continue to study the Word, the nucleus of life itself, but for now I have me. I have embraced my Jewish heritage for its spiritual rituals and the promise I made my earthly father to respect our name. I embrace my African heritage for my skin and hair and the wonderful features I was gifted with. I embrace my blackness, indelibly me.

I embrace my madness, also me. The Bible has said of Job's response, *"Naked I came from my mother's womb, and naked I will depart. The Lord gave and the Lord has taken away, may the name of the Lord be praised." Job* 1:21 *(NIV).* The chapter further went on to say that, *"In all this, Job did not sin by charging God with wrongdoing." v22 (NIV).* That is not to say I was not caught completely off guard with my last attempt at suicide. I couldn't believe I had done it. I knew better than to encroach on God's territory. Yet again

He had rescued me from the consequences of my illness.

It was while I was lying in the Intensive Care Unit attached to myriads of wires with an aid sitting at my side making sure my hands were above the sheets, that the full import of what I had done hit me. I realized that I had committed the cardinal sin, but then all the choirs of heaven burst forth singing, *"No one will be able to stand up against you all the days of your life. As I was with Moses, so I will be with you; I will never leave you nor forsake you." Jos. 1:5* (NIV) We are encouraged to remember how God led us in the past (as individuals and as His people) so we may have hope and wait on Him.

I am a perfectly woven tapestry of perfection and faults, for this I will borrow a thought from Paul after his pleading with the Lord, and the Lord responded, *"My grace is sufficient for you, for my power is made perfect in weakness."* So Paul said *"therefore I will boast all the more gladly about my*

weakness, so that Christ's power may rest on me".
2cor.12:9 (NIV). My body is subjected to domi-
nance but my spirit when intertwined with the
Light of Christ is indomitable. I can now face
life staring the tiger of my illness and trauma in
the eye, because now I know my nemesis. The
Spirit that dwells within has made a pussycat of
him. The eyes of the tiger no longer beguile me
with its power, inducing tears and doom in my
soul. The eyes now bring me a challenge of life,
a life I can either choose to live in triumph or
in defeat.

When the beast bears its teeth and growls in
response to my lack of fear, I do just what the
Lord instructs; *"I fear no evil, for you are with me;*
your rod and your staff, they comfort me." Ps.23:4 He
has also provided gifted doctors and therapists
to help me understand the nature and complex-
ities of my illness with talk and medication.

Tethering on the brink of madness is not my
desired perch, so medication will be my lot un-

til the Lord says otherwise. I welcome medical involvement; it's a small price to pay for a noise-less experience. I understand that the method might not be the preferred method for every-one. There are many approaches and the Lord will lead you into the one that is best for you.

The drummer still lends me His rod and His staff that comforts me. He stays with me when I can't meet with my friends because my battle wounds ache too much to be with peo-ple. He dries my tears when I cry for the little girl that has not quite grown up. I know these episodes are temporary; he had prepared me for these crying days. He told me I would carry the wounds, but not to worry, the battle would soon be over. In that Day He will vanquish the foe I had not seen, the one who had tried to take His music from me. Our foe's days are numbered. He knows it and is angry, not at me but at Him, because He never gave up on me.

The final words in the green book (Bible) my brother Valdez bought are these: *"He who testifies of these things says, 'Yes, I am coming soon."Rev.22:20(NIV).* I rest on the promise that in the New Jerusalem there will be no pain, no tears, no death, or illness. *"...Amen. Come, Lord Jesus. The grace of our Lord Jesus Christ be with God's people. Amen." Rev. 22:20,21 (NIV)*

Appendix: List of Resources

Because of the nature of this memoir I feel comfortable in sharing with you a list of organizations that were helpful in one way or the other. For more information you can call or write any of these organizations for free information. You can also find more information on their websites. Having faith in God requires that you take action. Be active in your search for peace and knowledge.

Mental Health

National Depressive and Manic Depressive Association (NDMDA) www.ndmda.org

NAMI FaithNet, faithnet.nami.org. Geared for those of faith.

Child and Adolescent Bipolar foundation
(CABF) www.bpkids.org

Mental Health Ministries
www.mentalhealthministries.org

National Alliance for the Mentally Ill (NAMI)
www.nami.org

National Foundation for depressive illness, Inc.
(NAFDI) www.depression.org

**National Depressive and Manic Depressive
Association (NDMDA)**
730 N. Franklin Street, Suite 501
Chicago, IL 60601-7204
1-800-826-3632
312-642-0049
Web site: http://www.ndmda.org

National Institute of mental Health (NIMH)
www.nimh.nih.gov

Information Resources and Inquiry

National Mental Health Association (MHA)
www.nmha.org

Rape, Abuse & Incest

Rape, Abuse & Incest National Network (RAINN) www.rainn.org

Survivors of Incest Anonymous, Inc (SIA) World Service Office www.siawso.org

The American Association for Suicide Prevention (AFSP) www.afsp.org

Child & Adolescent Bipolar Foundation (CABF)
1187 Willmette Avenue, PMB #331
Willmette, IL 60091
847-256-8525
Web site: http://www.bpkids.org

Job Accommodation Network (JAN)
A service of the US Department of Labor's Office of Disability
Employment policy

West Virginia University
P.O. Box 6080
Morgantown, WV 26506-6080
1-800-526-7234 (Voice or TTY)
Web site http://www.jan.wvu.edu/

American Association of Pastoral Counselors

http://www.aapc.org

Pastoral Counseling is a unique form of psychotherapy that uses spiritual resources as well as psychological understanding for healing and growth. The American Association of Pastoral Counselors (AAPC) represents and sets professional standards for over 3,000 Pastoral Counselors and 100 pastoral counseling centers in North America and around the world.

Author Qualifications
To Write This Book

Cheryl C. Silvera was an elementary school teacher for special education in New York City public school system. She holds certification from the University of the State of New York Education Department in Special Education. Earlier she earned her Master of Science Degree in Communications Design at Pratt Institute in Brooklyn, New York in 1997; her thesis is entitled *"Ethics awareness for the design student: based on spiritual values."* She was born in Jamaica West Indies to a family of non-practicing Sephardic Jews. Her first foray into the world of imaginings and study began at the Jamaica School of Art (now the Edna Manley School of Art) at the cultural Training Center, the Caribbean's only art school. In the 80's. She worked as a graphic designer for a popular design studio before being tapped by the country's leading advertising agency to become part of their staff. Taking a risk and branching out on her own, she started a book-binding, monogrammed subcontracting small business whose clients were hotels, insurance companies, travel agents and those interested in promoting their business. The attention that this business garnered brought forth a trump card in an offer to join the team of consultants to the Cottage Craft Organization which was *Under The Office of the Prime Minister.* Here she enjoyed a varied portfolio of fiber and fabrics. As a tribute to her personal work on her small business she was sponsored as a booth holder in the annual 'Women in Business' exposé at the Jamaica Pegasus Hotel 1987 giving credibility to contribution to small business.

She is a practicing Christian and attends a Bible believing church regularly where she finds spiritual guidance and renewal. One of her most memorable employment is working for the Hebrew Adventist Congregation starting and designing a program of sale and promotions for their health food ministry. Learning about and co-hosting the rituals of the Jewish festivals and holidays were an added bonus. Her creative talents are indoor gardening, acrylic painting and drawing in various media.

Glossary

Bells. Attached to the high priest's dress, and rung by striking against the knobs, shaped like pomegranates, which were hung near them.

Drum (toph). Shaped like a cask with bulging center, and was made of copper. It was placed in the Temple court and was used to call the priests to prayer, and could be heard from Jerusalem to Jericho.

Messianic Jew: Believes in the New Testament and that Jesus is the Messiah. According to Paul in Rev 21: 9-12 anyone who would come into the Messiah must necessarily enter through Israel (Jews or Gentile). Gentiles are grafted into the olive tree of remnant Israel. Rom. 11: 16-24.

Sackbut. A harp-like instrument of four strings with a triangular form.

Sephardic. Comes from the Hebrew word for Spain.

Shofar. The same as a horn (cut from a ram's horn). A trumpet.

Temple Choir. 2 Sam. 6:5 David chose 4000 musicians from the 38,000 Levites. By this means battles were won, cities conquered, mutinies quelled, diseases cured.

Timbrel. A form of tambourine, a narrow hoop covered with tightened skin and struck with the hand.

Yeshua. Means Salvation. (Jesus)